Triumph Motorcycles

Their Renaissance and the Hinckley Factory

Other Titles in the Crowood MotoClassics Series

Triumph Motorcycles

Their Renaissance and the Hinckley Factory

Johnny Tipler

THE CROWOOD PRESS

First published in 1997 by
The Crowood Press Ltd
Ramsbury, Marlborough
Wiltshire SN8 2HR

www.crowood.com

Revised paperback edition 2006

© Johnny Tipler 1997 and 2006

British Library Cataloguing-in-Publication Data
A catalogue record for this book is available from the British Library.

ISBN 1 86126 864 5
EAN   978 1 86126 864 8

Typeset by D&N Publishing
Lambourn Woodlands, Hungerford, Berkshire.

Printed and bound in Great Britain by CPI Bath.

Contents

A Modern History of the New Triumphs

1984	John Bloor founds the new company. Technicians begin work on new modular concept machines.
1988	Triumph acquires the 10-acre (4ha) site at Dodwell's Bridge industrial estate, Hinckley. The construction of the new factory begins.
1990	Production of the new Triumph range begins.
September 1990	The launch of six models – the Trident 750 and the Daytona 750 triple and the 1000 four, and the Trophy 900 triple and the 1200 four – at the Cologne Motorcycle Show in Germany.
February 1991	The first model goes into production: it is the Trophy 1200.
March 1991	The first batch off the line is exported to Germany. UK distribution soon follows.
June 1991	Production begins of the first new-generation triples: the Trident and Daytona 750 and the Trident and Trophy 900.
October 1991	Exports to the Netherlands, France and Australia.
January–June 1992	Distributors appointed in Italy, Spain, Switzerland and Japan.
October 1992	New models introduced at the Cologne Show are the Daytona 900, the Tiger enduro and the Sprint. The 5,000th bike leaves the Hinckley plant.
November 1992	At the Birmingham NEC Show, the 147bhp Daytona is launched. 'Too fast for the road,' bleats Tory MP.
February 1993	In snow and icy conditions, some forty German dealers take delivery of the first Daytona 900s and 1200s at Hinckley – and ride them back home.
March–May 1993	Sweden is among new markets receiving Triumph exports.
July 1993	10,000th bike leaves the Hinckley factory.
September 1993	Triumph launches the Speed Triple and the Daytona Super III at the Paris Motorcycle Show. There are now ten models in the line-up.
January 1994	The company makes its debut in the Canadian market at the Toronto Show.
February 1994	Planning permission is granted for the construction of a new factory on a 40-acre (16ha) site, half a mile (1km) from the present plant.

March 1994	A US subsidiary, Triumph Motorcycles America Ltd, is set up, with plans for a product launch the following year.
July 1994	The inaugural Speed Triple Challenge race is held at the Donington Park circuit.
October 1994	Triumph models go on sale in the USA. The Thunderbird classic roadster makes its debut at the Cologne Show, while Triumph France takes delivery of its 20,000th bike, a Speed Triple.
January 1995	The company introduces its range of specialized clothing and accessories under the Triple Connection banner.
April 1995	The Mobil One Speed Triple Challenge race series gets under way.
June 1995	Triumph Motorcycles America launches the Transatlantic Speed Triple Challenge race series. New distributors are appointed for South Africa and Singapore.
August 1995	The 30,000th new Triumph, a Thunderbird, leaves Hinckley bound for Australia.
September 1995	The Adventurer, a retro-styled cruiser, makes its debut at the Paris Salon, along with the radically facelifted Trophy 900 and 1200.
April 1996	Triumph Australia takes delivery of the 30,000th Triumph, a Trophy model.
September 1996	A new owners' club is established by the factory, known as the 'Riders' Association of Triumph', or RAT.
October 1996	Launch of the new supersports Daytona T595 and the café-racer Speed Triple T509 at the Cologne Show, pioneering fuel injection and taking alloy frame technology to new heights. Over 700 advance orders had already been taken by dealers for the Daytona.

Acknowledgements

Needless to say, this couldn't have been written without the collaboration of Triumph themselves, so I have to say a big thank-you to John Bloor for permission to carry out research and photography at the factory. My host was Bruno Tagliaferri, sales and marketing director, and he introduced me to all the right people so I could arrange interviews and have photos taken of the build process. So thanks to Bruno for all his assistance, to Anne Marrinan in PR for liaison and providing Speed Triple Challenge passes; to Robert Brown for the guided tours; to the supervisors, including Steve Whatnall and John Bradley; the team leaders, in particular Matt Jones, Guy Campton, Mark Thomas, Karl Orton, Nigel Burbage and Rob Miller; and everyone else at the factory for their helpful comments during my visits.

All factory shots were taken by Simon Clay, now partly freelance, although then working full time for the National Motor Museum. The black-and-white shots were laboriously printed by Sam Little in the Beaulieu dark room, and the archive material also came from Beaulieu. Other pictures were taken by me using Andy Robinson's camera equipment – for which thanks again, Andy.

You can't write about them without riding them, and I am especially grateful to Paul Barkshire and Barry Lynes, managers of Triumph's Norfolk and Suffolk dealership P.F.K. Ling's of Watton and Ipswich. They very kindly lent me a selection of new and nearly new Triumph demonstrators to ride, and Paul spent a morning talking me through the ups and downs of selling motorcycles, and Triumphs in particular.

Finally, I want to dedicate the book to my parents, Margaret and Don. My father is a big motorbike fan, and rode a Tiger 80 in the late 1930s, and during the early war years, a silver Tiger 100. Before going out to Burma he commuted from Lincoln to Pembrey on this machine – seizing it up once when the Castrol R lubricant proved too fine for the oil system and blew out. Not a chance of that happening nowadays!

Introduction

A decade on from my first encounter with the Hinckley factory, Triumph production has come on in leaps and bounds. A lot that seemed awe-inspiring and pioneering in the mid-1990s we now take for granted. Back then there was a real sense that these achievements might not endure, and certainly a feeling that we were witnessing something very special, precious even. In the meantime, much has been consolidated

When this book was first written, Triumph had just launched the new Daytona T595. This almost-finished example at the factory shows off the format of the seat subframe.

and the company is very much planted in the mainstream motorcycle manufacturing industry. So it's entirely fitting that my publisher, The Crowood Press, should reprint this book with an additional chapter to update the story. While the bulk of the book contains images pertaining to the original Jacknell Road factory, the final chapter brings us up to 2006. The thing to bear in mind is that Triumph's methodology, techniques and equipment didn't alter with the relocation of production, despite the introduction of new models; it's simply that the environment the company operates in is now on a much grander scale.

During the latter part of 1996 when I was researching and writing this book, Triumph was approaching the crest of a wave, having just launched and put into production its brand-new T595 Supersport and T509 Speed Triple models. It added extra zest to my research, and there was even more of a buzz around the factory and the dealers. The significance of the new models was not just that they could take on the best of the Japanese and the Italians and come out on top, but also that the company had the confidence to do it. It was proof that the renaissance was well and truly here to stay.

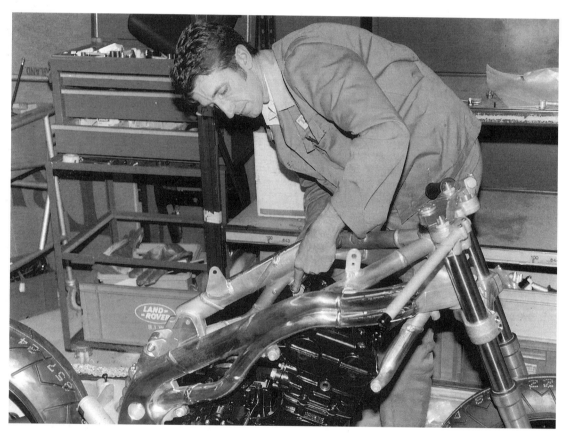

Chassis 2 team leader Guy Campton tightens the engine-mounting bolts on a T509 Speed Triple destined for the model's 1996 launch at the NEC Show.

Detail of the rear monoshock and single-sided swing-arm on the T509 Speed Triple.

In a sense, the old Triumph name is not relevant any more. In the main, people old enough to remember the Meriden days and before are not the ones buying the bikes today, and in fact the production system which creates the modern bikes is so far removed from Meriden as to be an entirely new operation. Even Triumph themselves are not especially interested in the marque's past, preferring to concentrate their energies on the future. You won't find much in the way of archives of nostalgia at Hinckley. So these fabulous machines could be just as effectively marketed as Vincents or Nortons, or whatever evocative name happened to be available. However, as yet only a small proportion of the British public is aware that Triumph is up and running again and building state-of-the-art worldclass motorcycles.

Apart from Morgan, no other specialist vehicle producer I have visited approaches the degree of self-sufficiency found at Triumph's Hinckley factory. The sense of completeness about the production cycle is most satisfying, and there is a definite buzz about the place. Morale is high amongst the predominantly young workforce, and with good reason: they have an excellent working environment, a sound relationship with management, and inter-factory communications are good. Most significantly, the machines they produce are first class, and a major reason for this is that the people who build them are well motivated.

Such is the popularity of Triumph bikes that they run as many as two factory tours every day. More than 40 per cent of the bikes' componentry is manufactured in house, probably more than any other maker. Only a relatively small number of items are sourced in Japan, simply because they cannot be found anywhere else. Motorcycle manufacture is a long way from the Meriden days, let alone Priory Street, and in most areas the technology employed at Hinckley is truly state-of-the-art. The new models are designed by computer-aided design – CAD – and certain components are constructed by computer-aided manufacturing, or CAM. For maximum efficiency the whole system works on the Japanese principle of Kan-Ban, whereby parts are supplied to the assembly line 'just in time' to fulfil orders, rather than the factory having to stockpile masses of idle components.

You can see the faceless banks of metal containers concealing the robotized CNC machine tools that create the pressings and hone the castings which go to make up the motorcycles, and although these are somewhat sanitized compared with the production

lines of old, there is no doubt as to their efficiency and precision. This aspect of the Triumph production process is not labour-intensive, with only a handful of technicians operating the machines. The majority of the workforce is involved in assembly, but here they have the very latest jigs and air tools to make life easier.

There might be little evidence of Triumph's past glories at the Hinckley plant, but they have managed to turn the marque's heritage to good marketing advantage. This is demonstrated by the qualified success of the classic Thunderbird and Adventurer models, which are decidedly 'retro' in spirit and appearance and hark back to the 'good old days' of post-war motorcycling when Triumphs could do no wrong. The fuel tanks are hand-decorated with enormous care by a signwriter – no decal stripes here.

Triumph motorcycles stand out in any company, whether they are classic bikes or

A Tiger at bay. Triumph's ability to venture into specialized markets with models such as the enduro demonstrates a confidence in its products and in its manufacturing methodology.

With over thirty dealers worldwide, the company is well placed for exports, and while travelling abroad during 1996, the author encountered several Triumphs, including a Daytona like this 1995 model.

new ones. In this book I focus on the modern ones, not merely because the history has already been written up and books are available on specific models from the past, but because the Hinckley-based company's rebirth is a fantastic achievement, and the manufacturing process a fascinating one. Modern Triumphs are classy machines, and have that extra helping of refinement over Japanese bikes. The one-colour liveries of the fared bikes define the shape of the machine far more eloquently than the multi-hued race-rep schemes frequently adorning Japanese bikes. Triumphs are, in

short, more grown up than most of the competition.

As Britain's roads become ever more congested and tempers quicken as progress slows, the motorcycle is now not merely the best way to enjoy travelling, but looking increasingly like the mode of transport of the future. In 1996, when I wrote the original text, I rode a Honda CBR600. Having penned this book, however, I simply had to have a Triumph of my own, so I bought a beautiful cherry-red 750 Trident. The lust for power and a fairing led me to stray from the Hinckley path and I bought a VFR800, but it wasn't long before I saw the error of my ways and I fell for a 955i Speed Triple. Everyone loves it, especially the children.

Sightings of new Triumphs on recent trips abroad were sufficiently memorable highlights to record here. Last summer I caught sight of a Trident in the southern Swedish university city of Lund, a black Daytona at Gothenburg, and a Tiger in Stockholm. And on the way to Portugal for Easter I had three encounters with Triumphs: the first was in Libourne, near Bordeaux, when a Frenchman tottered out of a dealer's forecourt in front of me on a yellow Daytona, presumably trying it on for size.

Later on I caught up with a German-registered Speed Triple at Zamora, close to the Spanish-Portuguese border. As we passed over a narrow road bridge, it was a wrench to take my eyes off the Triumph in order to gawp at the mighty River Duero in spectacular full spate. It wasn't until we were well and truly on the wrong road out of Zamora that I realized I had been wrong-footed, not so much by the poor signposting but by paying too much attention to the Speed Triple. And down at Resende on the Douro I was astonished to see a convoy of Triumphs, three Sprints, a Tiger and a Daytona.

My CBR600 proved as unreliable as its successor, the Trident, proved dependable. The VFR was as bland as the Speed Triple was exciting, which speaks volumes for Triumph products ranged against the popular wisdom concerning the best Japanese bikes.

An RAC patrol man rides a specially equipped Trident. If only he had been around the night the author's CBR600 broke down.

1 Origins of the Marque

There have been four major episodes of management in Triumph's long history. The long-lasting Siegfried Bettmann era endured from 1885 to 1936, followed by the period under Edward Turner from 1936 to 1973; then the short-lived Norton-Villiers-Triumph phase and the Meriden workers' co-operative between 1973 and 1984; and finally the modern-day John Bloor period which began in 1984, and which forms the major thrust of this book. The story of Triumph has been told already, most recently by Ivor Davies, and by others in specific model histories, but any book about a company needs an historical overview, and the following chapters set the stage for Hinckley.

In 1883, Siegfried Bettmann arrived in Britain from Nuremberg. He took on agencies for products of several foreign companies, notably the White Sewing Machine Co of Cleveland Ohio, which went on to specialize in truck manufacture. The bicycle was in its infancy, and Bettmann teamed up with Birmingham manufacturer William Andrews to make a cycle which he named the Triumph. Since Coventry was the heart of the bicycle industry, Bettmann and his engineer partner Mauritz Schulte set up a factory in 1887, in premises rented from the mayor in Much Park Street in the city's Earl's Court district, to manufacture the machines. The Triumph Cycle Company soon went public, its shares underwritten by the Dunlop Tyre Company to the tune of £45,000.

MOTORCYCLE PRODUCTION BEGINS

In 1896 Triumph began experimenting with powered cycles, and went into production with its first motorcycle in 1902. This was subsequently known as Number One, and was basically a strengthened cycle frame carrying a 239cc Minerva engine mounted on the front down-tube and bottom bracket. It had a mechanical inlet valve and Longuemare spray carburettor, and a drive-belt worked on a pulley within the rear wheel rim, with a fuel tank slung below the cross-bar. The front brake was a regular bicycle stirrup type. Power output was 2.25hp at 1,500rpm, and its top speed was 25mph (40kph). Triumph also used British-made JAP and Fafnir engines, but the Belgian engine was reckoned to be superior to British offerings at the time. In 1904 Triumph adopted the 'Werner' position, placing the engine within the triangle of the main frame.

Priory Street: Pre-war Triumphs

Triumph were catching up, and in 1906 from its newly acquired Priory Street premises, under the guidance of Schulte and works manager and chief designer Charles Hathaway, it was producing its very own machines, powered by its own engines. Again, it was based on an uprated bicycle frame with rack-mounted battery and direct belt-drive to the rear wheel. The motor was a 3hp

Looking little more than a motorized bicycle, the very first Triumph was made in 1902 and powered by a Belgian 2.25hp Minerva engine.

TWN

Triumph had an associate company based in Bettmann and Schulte's original home town of Nuremberg. TWN stood simply for 'Triumph Werke Nürnberg', and was established in 1903 as an offshoot of the Triumph Cycle Co.

For the first few years, TWN machines were virtually identical to the Coventry ones, although the company logo was rather different; the rusticated art nouveau letters were transfixed by a push-rod. The TWN Knirps – or 'Nipper' – of 1914 was a 3hp two-stroke directly related to the Triumph Junior. This model went into production after the war in 1920 with a 276cc engine.

By 1929 the family resemblance had disappeared, although TWN carried on producing motorcycles until 1957, when it moved over to typewriter manufacture. After World War II, it resumed production with pre-war designs, coming out with the 'split singles' such as the BDG 125 in 1949. The principle of this arrangement was that the inlet ports were located in one cylinder and the exhaust ports in another, sharing a common combustion chamber and, theoretically at any rate, an improved combustion cycle.

---

single-cylinder side-valve 363cc unit, and the first of its type with the mainshaft running in ball bearings. Although the standard ignition was by accumulator, a Simms-Bosch magneto was available for an extra £5. Hathaway also designed and patented the horizontal spring fork, which remained a unique Triumph feature for a long time to come.

Bore and stroke of the 'Three Horse' model were increased to 453cc in 1907, and bored up to 476cc the following year. An advancement was the adjustable pulley on the crankshaft which gave a better ratio for climbing steep hills. The only drawback was

After coming second in the first-ever Isle of Man TT race – single-cylinder class – in 1907, Jack Marshall won the event in 1908. He averaged 40.49mph (65kph) on a 3.5hp model.

that the belt itself had to be shortened by means of a removable section in order for the process to work.

In 1907 Triumph featured on the sporting map too, with Jack Marshall bringing his 3.5hp model home in second place behind Charlie Collier's Matchless in the single cylinder class of the very first Isle of Man TT event. Marshall won the class in 1908, setting the fastest lap at 42.48mph (68.3kph). Other Triumph riders came in third, fourth, fifth, seventh and tenth, which was an impressive demonstration indeed, prompting Triumph to offer a TT Racer in its 1911 catalogue. This race-rep featured the drop bars and low-slung saddle of the authentic race machines, footrests instead of pedals, and higher pulley ratios. In the 1911 TT, eight out of eight Triumphs finished.

Also in 1911 came a significant innovation with the introduction of the 499cc Hub Clutch model, making it no longer necessary to bump start the bike because a plate clutch was introduced. This was fitted in the rear

Given the variable pulley of the 3.5hp model, which provided alternative ratios, this 1908 rider appears to be savouring the prospect of the Brooklands hill climb.

Proudly displayed before a fake Arcadian backdrop, this 494cc model of 1909 has modified front forks, fuel tank, tool box and luggage carrier.

hub and operated by a heel-and-toe pedal to the right of the engine. It was also consequently possible to bring the machine to a halt without having turned the engine off. Pedals and chain sprockets were still fitted, but the frame had by now become a flatter diamond shape, moving away from the former bicycle geometry, while the front forks incorporated Triumph's unique rocking spring system. They were hinged at the base of the head set and controlled from above by a horizontal spring fitted on the handlebar stem. The system was quite satisfactory, bearing in mind the machines were now capable of nearly 50mph (80kph).

Bettmann was made chairman of the Standard Motor Company in 1911, a strange portent of the acquisition of the Triumph car company by Standard in 1944. As a councillor, Bettmann had long been involved in the city's administration, and by 1913 he was Mayor of Coventry. A measure of his civic popularity and influence is that one of his 'good works', the Prince of Wales'

Fund, accumulated £8,000 – a huge sum of money then – in a matter of weeks.

Triumphs in World War I

By this time Triumph's reputation was so firmly established that when World War I broke out, Triumph was asked by the War Office to supply 100 motorcycles for army use at the front. They complied, and the requisitioning officer, Col. Claude Holbrook, went on to become manager of Triumph as Schulte was pensioned off for some £15,000. Some 30,000 Triumph motorcycles went into service during the war; they were 4hp Type H models, so reliable that, despite the omnipresent belt-drive, they earned the epithet 'Trusty Triumphs'. It was no coincidence that the firm's telegram code was 'Trusty Coventry', which it retained to the bitter end. Power-plant of the Model H was the by now standard 550cc 4hp side-valve unit allied to a countershaft three-speed Sturmey Archer gearbox and chain primary drive.

A simpler machine than the Type H was the 225cc two-stroke Junior – nicknamed the Baby Triumph – which came out in 1913. It was rather overlooked as a consequence of the Great War, but continued to be listed in the Triumph catalogue until 1925. It was produced under licence for a short time as a 269cc machine by Ignatz Schwinn in Chicago, alongside the Henderson Model K and the Excelsior 20R.

Another machine which was not developed because of the war was a 600cc vertical twin, which existed as a prototype in 1913. The idea was not new to Triumph, who had experimented with a Bercley in 1909. Designed by Schulte and Hathaway, the 1913 model was a side-valve unit with 180-degree crankshaft housed in a horizontally split crankcase and exterior flywheel. Unlike later Triumph twins, the pistons would rise and fall alternately, but as with more modern big twins, the machine was troubled by vibrations.

Post-war Triumphs

Triumph's post-war 5.5hp Type SD model was not fundamentally different from the 550cc Model H, although two important developments were the replacement of belt drive by an all-chain system, and a transmission shock absorber was incorporated in the clutch – hence spring-drive or 'SD' – to provide a smoother drive. Pedals were banished, and the 242lb (109kg) machine was fitted with a kick-start.

Two years later, in 1922, Triumph had a winner on its hands with the 499cc Type IR 'Fast Roadster.' What was significant about this machine was its cylinder head configuration, which consisted of four pushrod-actuated overhead valves with centrally positioned spark plug. The head had been designed by piston and combustion chamber specialists Ricardo & Co, with both sets of valves arranged at 90 degrees to one another. There

This 1923 Triumph 'Spring Drive' 550cc machine rounds the Cross during the 1955 Banbury Run; the clutch now incorporated a shock absorber for the transmission.

The 500cc ohv type IR Fast Roadster of 1922 was popularly known as the Riccy, after cylinder head and piston specialist Harry Ricardo. Frank Halford set many world speed records on a Riccy during the 1920s.

was a single inlet manifold from the carburettor, but exhaust emissions passed away down two separate pipes. The piston was aluminium, running in a bore machined from steel billet, and power output was 20bhp, making a top speed of 75mph (120kph) possible. The IR's frame and cycle components were directly descended from the Model H, although the druid-pattern girder forks were a slight improvement.

The Type IR was known affectionately as the 'Riccy', after Harry – later Sir Harry – Ricardo, whose engineering talents with aero and car engine development were well known. Triumph reverted to concentrate on two-valve models from 1924, and Ricardo's advanced concepts were neglected for some thirty-five years until Honda brought them back with its 1960s racing machines. Nowadays we tend to take multi-valve technology

for granted, but the principles of improved fuel flow, reduced reciprocating mass – allowing higher revs – and more efficient combustion and exhaust were not widely appreciated in Ricardo's day.

The Type R model was campaigned widely in competition, and Walter Brandish took second place in the 1922 Senior TT on his Riccy, averaging 56.52mph (90.9kph). Frank Halford – later to become managing director of de Havilland aircraft engines – set a number of world records on a Riccy. Halford left the 'flying mile' (1.6km) at 83.91mph (135kph), the 'fifty miles' (80km) at 77.27mph (124.3kph), and the 'one hour' at 76.74mph (123.4kph).

Only the appearance of the all-new 500cc Type TT in 1927 displaced the Type IR Riccy from the Triumph range. Meanwhile, the market in the early 1920s for road-going rather than racing bikes had slackened, so in 1924 Bettmann had brought out a more pedestrian machine, the low-budget side-valve 494cc Type P, in order to entice would-be Triumph owners. At almost half the cost of a regular SD – just £42 17s 6d – it was priced to sell, and orders flooded in. The factory was stretched to cope, and production flowed at the rate of around 1,000 bikes a week, with over 20,000 units built. However, the economies made with the Type P's spec brought many complaints from dissatisfied customers. Clutch and big-end failure were common, while the inadequacy of the asbestos string-and-pulley front brake caused much discontent; matters were only improved with the creation of a superior Mark 2 version.

The opposite side of the coin, specification-wise, was the 346cc Type LS, a single-cylinder machine featuring a three-speed gearbox in unit with the side-valve engine. As well as a gear primary drive, it had a steel and copper all-metal clutch mechanism and force-fed lubrication system. Originally launched with drum brakes front and rear, the back brake on production models was nothing more than a dummy belt rim. However, the overall specification was way ahead of the current state-of-the-art in 1924, and only a few were actually sold. Buyers were more tempted, *en masse*, by the less complex, bargain-basement Type P model.

Demand for personal transport in the early 1920s was keen, and it meant that motorcycles faced stiff competition not only from the now massed-produced car firms, but also the three-wheeler cyclecars. These were halcyon days for firms like Morgan, who had a variety of different models available. Against Bettmann's judgement, the cycle-producing side of the firm was sold to Coventry Cycles and, in 1923, Triumph went into car production with the 10/20hp Super Seven light car, a competitor with the Austin 7. The car was designed by a talented array

of engineers and draughtsmen including S. F. Edge, A. A. Sykes, Walter Belgrove and Arthur Alderson of Lea Francis.

As the Riccy's popularity dwindled, it was superseded in 1927 by the two-valve Model TT. The engine was designed by Brooklands racer Victor Horsman, and featured a twin-port overhead-valve head, enclosed lubricated valve gear and roller-bearing rockers. There was a three-speed gearbox with traditional crossover drive. The hub brakes were of the expanding internal type front and rear, while new-fashioned front forks incorporated large fabric-friction discs and steering damper.

Publicity poster featuring the 1929 Model ST, an advanced twin port ohv single-cylinder machine based on a cradle frame and saddle tank. The carefree passenger sits on the padded luggage rack.

By now the motorcycle was beginning to look more like the modern machine rather than a vintage motorized bicycle. Like the ST, the 498cc Model CN of 1929 used a cradle frame and tear-drop profile fuel tank.

THE PAGE COLLECTION

While car manufacture forged ahead, motorcycle production continued at the original Priory Street factory, but the depression bit deep in 1930. Sales were down by 30 per cent, and for the first time this century the company paid no dividend on its ordinary shares. Needless to say, other makes were going through hard times as well, and one consequence was the arrival of Valentine ('Val') Page, former chief designer at JAP engines in Tottenham, and recruited by Triumph in 1932, along with Harry Perrey from the rival Ariel concern, then in financial difficulties. Among Page's claims to fame were the power-plants for the Brough Superior SS80 and SS100 machines, and at JAP he produced a 250cc engine which could scream at 8,000rpm, a rare beast indeed in the 1920s.

Val Page treated the Triumph catalogue to a clean sheet, creating a completely new range from 250cc, 350cc and 500cc ohv singles, through 350cc and 550cc side-valve singles to a 650cc ohv vertical twin. There were 147cc ohv lightweights as well. The singles were well-made and proved enormously durable, remaining in production for some five years. The valve gear in the twin-port head was completely enclosed and mechanically lubricated, while long overdue four-speed gearboxes were introduced, with shift to the right-hand side of the tank. A foot-operated gear lever was available for an extra £1. Magdyno lighting was fitted, and the 249cc base model 2/1 sold for £53.

There were three variations on the 500cc model, known as the 5/2, the 5/5 and the 5/10, the latter being a racing bike. Apart from that one, all the singles shared a similar appearance, which meant that smaller capacity machines were rather beefier than their actual performance capability. The same is true today of certain Japanese bikes in the small capacity classes which are deliberately styled to look like their bigger siblings.

The Page-designed 6/1 pushrod 650cc vertical twin was not as popular as the singles, although it was every bit as well conceived. It was a sturdy-looking bike, with heavy-duty duplex cradle-frame chassis,

A German subsidiary was set up in 1903, called Triumph Werke Nürnberg (TWN), and the Nüremberg factory made virtually identical models to the Coventry plant – like this 1930 ST model – until production ceased in 1957. Whether it is acceptable to be smoking a pipe when refuelling is another matter ...

girder front forks to match, and a substantial pair of mudguards. The parallel cylinders were set at 360 degrees, with a gear-driven single camshaft located within the casting behind the block, working the valves by unequal length pushrods. There was a Y-shaped induction manifold, and the gearbox was bolted directly in unit with the engine. There was no intermediate gear, so the helical gear primary drive ran the engine backwards. Some of these features would be taken up after World War II by Norton and BSA.

The 6/1 was said to be 'bullet-proof', and achieved a degree of fame in 1934 when TT ace Tommy Spann lapped Brooklands at 105mph (169kph) in a bid to win *The Motor Cycle* magazine's trophy for the first British multi-cylinder machine to cover 100 miles (160km) in the hour. However, magneto failure handed the accolade to Ginger Wood riding the New Imperial 500 V-twin on the same day, averaging 102.21mph (164.43kph). These were times when breaking records mattered, and the more obscure the better.

At Brooklands the previous year, a 6/1 650cc twin took the prestigious Maudes Trophy (awarded annually for the most significant achievement by a production machine) for completing the ISDT Six Days Trial and covering 500 miles (805km) in less than 500 minutes – with sidecar attached. This said something about the real strength of the 650cc twin, and its function as a sidecar hauler was probably uppermost in Page's mind when he designed the bike. It could actually be bought as a combination with sidecar attached. The production life of the 6/1 was destined to be over by 1936, however, as other matters were brought to bear on company fortunes.

Siegfried Bettmann, who had seen not only Triumph but the motor industry as a whole grow from absolutely nothing, had by now been rather overtaken by business developments: in 1933 he was sidelined by more progressive financial personalities behind the scenes, and Col. Claude Holbrook was made managing director. Holbrook's heart was not in the small cars Triumph had been producing in some quantity – 17,000 Super Sevens in seven years – and one of his first projects as director was the Triumph Gloria Dolomite. In effect it was to be a Coventry-built version of Alfa Romeo's starkly beautiful 8C 2300 Monza sports car, which in straight eight 2.3- and 2.6-litre form scored numerous competition successes in the early 1930s. As a reciprocal deal, Alfa had the rights to produce Triumph's 6/1 vertical twin, but the arrangement rather fizzled out with only three Gloria Dolomites built. The car plant prepared to relocate to Coventry's Holbrook district, where other models such as the Southern Cross, Dolomite and Vitesse would carry the company's banner. Powered by Coventry Climax engines from 1933 to 1937, they were clad in Triumph's own bodies as well as Tickford and Cross and Ellis. With Donald Healey as technical director, several competition successes were achieved. This was of little help to Triumph motorcycles, which on 22 January 1936 was sold to John Young Sangster of Ariel for just over £41,000.

ARIEL'S LEADER

As a motorcycle manufacturer, Ariel's origins were almost identical with those of Triumph, going back to 1902 – and with an ancestry stretching to wagon wheel manufacture in 1847. Ariel Cycles became a subsidiary of Charles Sangster and S. F. Edge's Cycle Components Ltd in 1898, making a de Dion engined three-wheeler the same year.

Ariel motorcycles came to prominence in 1926 with a range of machines powered by

557cc side-valve and 496cc ohv engines, designed by Val Page. In 1930 Ariel came out with the Edward Turner-designed 497cc Square Four, a machine which would endure, with revisions, until 1959. By 1932, however, Ariel was broke and foundering in the depression, and in a curious management buy-out, was rescued by Jack Sangster.

Meticulous, courteous and amiable, Sangster – or 'JS', as he became known – was born in 1896, son of Charles, the director and general manager of Ariel's parent company Components Ltd. After serving in World War I, JS became production manager at Rover cars, designing the flat-twin air-cooled engine for the Rover 8. Sangster left Rover in 1922 to work for his father at Ariel, where the flat-twin engine design was pressed into service. However, the Ariel Nine and Ten cars were no match price-wise for the mass-produced vehicles of Austin and Morris. Ariel concentrated on motorcycles, with Val Page as chief designer, and in 1929 Sangster brought in Edward Turner whose vision went a long way to making Ariel – and later Triumph – models so successful. With Page, Turner and Bert Hopwood in the design office, Ariel's fortunes looked set to prosper – but as it turned out, this trio's designs had more significance later on for Triumph, as well as BSA and Norton.

When Triumph Motorcycles was put up for sale, Jack Sangster was encouraged by Edward Turner to buy it. He bought the name Triumph Engineering – registered long ago but never actually used – with a lease for the plant and factory premises and an agreement to sell spare parts on commission. The company's capital value was registered at £21,000 on 25 February 1936.

Bettmann, by now aged seventy, had resigned from Triumph, but Sangster made him chairman of the new Triumph motorcycle concern. Not only would Bettmann have been delighted that 'his' company was secure once more, but his kudos among suppliers meant the business continued to enjoy good component supply. As well as being a key employer in the city, Bettmann put back much of his success into the community through a number of charities. A freemason, he had led a varied life, including being president of the British Cycle and Motor Cycle Manufacturers and Traders' Union. He wrote several books based on experiences in South Africa, India and Egypt, and died aged eighty-eight in 1951.

EDWARD TURNER'S TENURE

When Val Page went to Triumph in 1932, Turner became chief designer at Ariel, and when Sangster acquired Triumph in 1936, he took on that role there, too. Equally significantly, he was appointed general manager as well.

Edward Turner was born in London in 1901, and after serving as a wireless operator in the merchant navy in World War I, he set up as a Velocette dealer and service agent in Peckham, south-east London. Working from a corner shop, Turner designed and built his own 350cc motorcycle. His quest to mass-produce the bike led him to Ariel, where Jack Sangster quickly signed him up as a draughtsman. One of Turner's achievements was the popularization of Page's Red Hunter range, accomplished simply by using bright colours for the tanks and chrome-plating the exhaust pipes. His beefy Square Four stole the show at its launch at Olympia in 1930.

With the acquisition of Triumph, it was clear to Turner that the cosmetic job which had worked for the Red Hunters was the way to go with the Page singles, the 2/1, the 3/2 and the 5/5. They were each given a name: the 250cc Tiger 70, the 350cc 80 and the 500cc 90, which, accompanied by a touch of chrome and bright paintwork, gave them an instant new lease of life. There was a real resurgence of interest in Triumph, and in order to shift product, the sales operation was redefined, with the country divided into three territories, and no factory-based sales manager.

At about this time, the American connection was established. Bill Johnson, a Californian lawyer, bought an Ariel Square Four while on honeymoon in Hawaii, and took the bike home with him. He broached the subject of a distributorship with Edward Turner, and was given the West Coast franchise. When Turner went over to Triumph, Johnson added that make to the stocklist of his Pasadena-based Johnson Motors Inc. dealership as well, and it was to be the start of a highly important source of custom for the company.

THE SPEED TWIN

In the 29 July 1937 issue of *The Motor Cycle*, the year after Ariel's takeover, Triumph launched Turner's *pièce de résistance*, the Speed Twin. It was less than two years since production of the 6/1 had ended, and the new machine had little in common with the old vertical twin. The Speed Twin engine's appeal lay in its lightness, which at 378lb (171kg) – 5lb (2.2kg) less than the Tiger 90 single, in whose frame it was fitted – enabled it to reach a top speed of 93mph (149kph), while at £75, it was only £5 dearer than the Tiger 90. It was also a slightly narrower bike than the Tiger 90. With its twin pipes tucked neatly under the engine, it was possible for the Speed Twin to be leaned over at extreme angles during cornering – more than 45 degrees was said to be possible before the

The legendary Speed Twin was designed by Edward Turner and launched in 1937. Its compact engine was the model for all British twins for fifty years, and its 93mph (149.6kph) top speed was matched by its smart amaranth colour scheme and hand-painted tank detailing.

footrests scraped the ground. Despite its 360-degree configuration, the Speed Twin ran very smoothly, thanks to its understressed 63mm × 80mm engine and 7:1 compression. It developed 27bhp at 6,300rpm.

The block and head were of cast iron, and the single-throw crank had a central flywheel, split alloy con-rods and white metal-lined big-end caps. Twin camshafts were located ahead of and behind the block, while valve gear was mounted in separate alloy casings bolted to the head, and operated by pushrods housed in chrome tubes running between the cylinders. The pistons went up and down together, an arrangement which Turner believed provided better torque and efficient carburation than a twin with a two-throw crank, and better balance than a single of similar capacity.

The inlet camshaft pinion also drove the Lucas Magdyno and the double-plunger oil pump. Any decrease in oil pressure could be monitored by a nipple on the timing cover. An instrument panel set in Bakelite plastic was mounted on the tank top, and included a three-position light switch, ammeter and oil pressure gauge. The standard finish for the Speed Twin was a gorgeous shade of maroon known as amaranth – the Italian *amaranto* – with chrome tank, exhaust pipe, headlight and wheel rims, plus gold coach-lines and amaranth-coloured panels on the tank sides. The wheel-rim centres – 20in rear, 19in front – were similarly decorated, and the overall effect was quite dramatic.

Such was the performance potential of the Speed Twin that competition success was not far away. In 1938, the Speed Twin captured the Maudes Trophy, which consisted of a timed run between Land's End and John O'Groats, as well as high-speed lappery of Brooklands. Also participating in this event was the prototype of a bike launched in 1939, the sporting version of the Speed Twin called the Tiger 100.

The excellence of this silver-liveried Speed Twin came as a revelation to motorcyclists used to rather plodding singles. My father used one during the early 1940s for long-distance cross-country commuting and considered it to be first class. Author and former Triumph publicity manager Ivor Davies recalls '... after the single-cylinder 80, the Speed Twin felt like a Ferrari ...'. Its acceleration and quiet running, together with the important reliability factor, made it a very desirable machine. An early sales coup was the Speed Twin's selection by the London Metropolitan Police's motorcycle fleet in 1938. In fact it almost caused the demise of the big single, and set the scene for British parallel twin production in the post-war period, and indeed, served as the basis for the Triumph range for more than forty years.

The Speed Twin format was used in the 250cc, 350cc (3T), 500cc (5T), 650cc (6T) and 750cc engines, and rival manufacturers were considerably handicapped by Triumph's patents and took years to catch up. After World War II, a variety of ploys was adopted. Matchless installed a crankshaft centre bearing, ostensibly to iron out vibrations, while both BSA and Norton adopted the single camshaft layout of the Page-designed 6/1. Ariel, acquired by BSA in 1944, soldiered on with the Square Four until the 498cc and 646cc parallel twins of the 1950s. The model which probably came closest to the Speed Twin was Royal Enfield's 500 of 1948 which remained popular through the 1950s.

Bert Hopwood

Another seminal figure in Triumph's history – and indeed, in the story of the motor cycle – was Bert Hopwood. When Val Page left Ariel for Triumph, Hopwood succeeded him as chief draughtsman, and having worked closely with Edward Turner, it was logical to accompany him with the move to Triumph in 1936. As design assistant, Hopwood played a key role in the gestation of the Speed Twin. After the war he went to work for Norton, switching to BSA in 1949, then seven years later returning to Norton. By 1961, Hopwood was back at Triumph as deputy managing director. Here, in the late 1960s, he worked with development engineer Doug Hele on the creation of the three-cylinder Trident model. As a racing machine, the Trident was invincible, winning the TT 750 Production class in 1969 and 1970. As deputy managing director of BSA's Automotive Division, he was in a good – if that is the right word – position to observe the demise of the British motorcycle industry, and after his retirement he described the phenomenon in his book *Whatever Happened to the British Motorcycle Industry?* – which is essential reading for industrialists and bike fans alike.

Early Speed Twins

The design was clearly a successful one, and progress was swift. To start with, the early Speed Twins were known as 'six-stud' models, a reference to the bolts which secured the cylinder block to the crankcase. After running flat out they were prone to come undone, but by the following year a thicker block flange and an extra couple of studs had been added, and with this 'eight-stud' model the problem was cured. At the same time, girder forks were replaced by telescopics. Later on would come 650 and 750 versions.

The Tiger 100 of 1939 was the sports derivative of the Speed Twin, having polished ports, forged slipper pistons and a higher 8:1 compression ratio, and it replaced the Tiger 90 in the Triumph range. Its finish was equally as smart as the Speed Twin, and it featured a pair of megaphone-type silencers. At £80, it was £5 more expensive than the regular Speed Twin. From then on, Turner

would introduce a new touring model, and follow it a year later with a sporting model, although in years to come, owners would be able to up-spec their Speed Twins with high performance kits. In 1939, engine development chief Freddie Clarke equalled the 750cc class record at Brooklands on a Tiger 100 bored out to 503cc, leaving it for all time (because of the abandonment of the circuit) at 118.02mph (189.89kph).

THE WAR YEARS

As early as 1938 it was becoming obvious that there would be war, and the Ministry of Defence issued all the bike manufacturers with a specification for a machine for the military. It had to be over 250cc and under 250lb (113kg) in weight. Edward Turner's design was the 350cc twin, using a three-speed gearbox, and mounted in a lightweight frame using girder forks and equipped with an alternator for the lights – a motor industry first; it was designated the Model 3TW. After trials it was approved, and fifty units went into production.

At the outbreak of hostilities in 1939, the War Office requisitioned all available motorcycles for military use, and it mattered not what the specification was. Some were more suitable than others, and there was consternation among hard-bitten dispatch riders when they were issued with archaic 250cc BSA side-valve machines. Any finished product at the Priory Street factory was requisitioned with immediate effect, and all 350s and over which were still going down the line were bought up, totalling some 1,400 bikes in just the first six weeks of the war. Soldiers who received Tiger 100s were indeed fortunate, because the War Office specified a 350cc side-valve unit.

By January 1940 military demand had slackened, and production reverted to the domestic market for a while. A batch of 500cc side-valve machines went to the French services, while production was gradually given over to military equipment, including aircraft and tank components. These included links for tank tracks, and a winch for target-towing aircraft, powered by the 500cc Speed Twin motor. Later on, this engine also powered a portable generator for the radar units in Lancaster and Halifax heavy bombers. By May 1940 the 'Phoney War' was over, and Triumph set about making military 3TWs at the rate of 300 units a week.

Being an industrial city at the heart of the British economy and crucial to the entire war effort, Coventry was clearly an important target for German bombers, and a raid in October 1940 hit the enamelling shop, halting production for a few days as an unexploded bomb was removed. Then disaster struck on the night of 14 November 1940, when the centre of Coventry was reduced to rubble by a 400 bomber raid. Along with the mediaeval cathedral, Triumph's Priory Street factory was blitzed, with but a handful of the 3TWs completed and the remainder broken amongst a tangled mass of girders. Night-shift workers were lucky to escape unscathed in air-raid shelters, although the city sustained over 1,500 casualties that night.

With its entire production facility destroyed, Triumph began recovering whatever plant could be made serviceable, and it was installed in a former foundry in Warwick which was dubbed the Tin Tabernacle, a reference to a chapel on the site, clad in sheets of corrugated iron. Eventually, a fair amount of machinery was salvaged and incredibly, they were making motorcycles again by June 1941, consisting of side-valve and ohv 350s. The ohv 3HV had rocker boxes integral with the head, unlike the 343cc Tiger 80 where the alloy rocker boxes were separate. The chief drawback to these machines was that no air cleaner was fitted to

the Amal carburettor, so in desert theatres of war, the internals were quickly damaged by dust and sand.

Interestingly, even as the plant lay in ruins Turner was corresponding, in upbeat mood, with his agent Bill Johnson in California, confidently predicting fulfilment of orders and virtually denying there had ever been any bomb damage. There was a two-way crossover of Triumph parts. Johnson was doing his bit by sending over supplies of batteries and tyres, and crucially, Turner was furnishing him with gear components – a mysteriously large amount considering just how many units Johnson had actually sold by mid-1941. Turner and Johnson were even then considering post-war sales plans, as well as the prospects for the motor-scooter.

The two men's correspondence also indicates at an early date in the war – August 1941 – the perceived potential folly of Hitler's invasion of Russia, and an awareness of the Japanese military threat, pre-Pearl Harbor. Admitting the blitz damage, Turner waxes buoyantly to Johnson about the revival of Triumph fortunes and how good the sales climate for Triumph might be in post-war USA.

Although much of the ruins of the old Priory Street factory were left, it had been decided by the management – without Turner, who spent most of 1942 and 1943 with BSA – and the city fathers of Coventry, that a new factory should be built on the outskirts of the city. Work began on a greenfield site at Meriden, just off the A45, in July 1941, with production under way a little over a year later. The new plant and production line was bang up to date, and by 1944, output had reached 11,000 units, with attendant spares also being manufactured. In all, Triumph made 49,700 motorcycles for the armed forces during World War II, which was quite an achievement considering the destruction of the factory.

2   The Post-War Years

Paradoxically, war has a positive effect on technological innovation and development, despite the destruction and misery wrought by its products. However, the main benefit to Triumph Engineering during World War II was the construction of its new Meriden plant, even though it was equipped with archaic belt-driven machine tools salvaged from Priory Street, rather than any real advance in motorcycle design. Having been concentrating on the war effort, no new models were imminent; besides, the Speed Twin and Tiger 100 were still the pace-setters. Irishman Ernie Lyons emphasized that point by trouncing the Norton hoards in the wet to win the 1946 Manx Grand Prix on a works' Freddie Clarke-prepared Tiger 100. It spawned a short run of replicas soon afterwards. Prospects for overseas markets, especially in the US and Australia, looked promising. American servicemen stationed in Britain and Europe discovered the more sporting handling of British machines, and all of a sudden there was a glut of Harley Davidsons and Indians on the secondhand market.

Edward Turner held the view that the British motorcycle industry needed to satisfy five distinct markets, ranging from a moped and junior motorbike up to 150cc, then light sports and touring machines of 250 or 350cc, with high performance machines topping the range at between 500 and 1,000cc. Although this was not so far removed from the pre-war divisions, Triumph itself only came to address the commuter market with its scooters of the late 1950s, and its small capacity T15 Terrier of 1952 and T20 Tiger Cub of 1954 were as much sports-orientated as utility machines. Apart from the Cub derivatives, Triumph was always strongest in the medium- to large-capacity segments.

Broadly speaking, post-war Triumphs are identified by the following categories: pre-unit construction twins (1946–62), which encapsulates the T100 Tiger and early Thunderbird models; small unit-construction twins (1957–74) such as the T100A Tiger and the Daytona from the early sixties; single-cylinder machines (1953–74) such as the Terrier and Tiger Cub; large unit-construction twins (1963–75) such as the Thunderbird and the Bonneville; triples (1968–76), which were the T160 Trident and the short-lived Hurricane; the Meriden co-operative and Devon-built big twins, mostly Bonnevilles produced between 1976 and 1988; and then the main thrust of this book, the Hinckley triples and fours from 1991 onwards.

Meanwhile it was the pre-war 3T, the 5T Speed Twin and the Tiger 100 which carried Triumph over into the post-war era, with much of their componentry in common. The 350cc twin 3T *de luxe* made development work on the blitzed 3TW a reality, but the single-cylinder 3H model was never built. The main development was the switch to telescopic front forks and the abandonment of girder forks. Headlight lenses were now convex rather than flat, and in 1947 came the introduction of optional rear suspension in the shape of a sprung hub. This was interchangeable with the regular wheel, which was preferred by most riders over the less predictable undulations of the sprung hub version, and it bore no comparison with the swing arm suspension which would come later. Also optional at this time were close- or wide-ratio gear sets. The 3T lost its long through-studs for head and block, receiving the Speed Twin short studs for the block, and bolts for the head.

In 1949 a significant styling advance was instigated by Turner and Jack Wickes, his personal assistant and stylist: this was the nacelle which surrounded the head-stock on top of the forks. This contained the head-light, and the instrument panel consisting of speedo, ammeter, switches for lights, cut-out and steering damper knob, and it gave the machines a more streamlined appearance, which for the time being was unique to Triumph. The tank-top now came with a chrome baggage grid, while the oil pressure gauge was replaced by a tell-tale on the pressure release valve. The following year the logo on the side of the tank changed, having a horizontal four-bar background, and the cosmetics were much simplified. A bayonet-type filler cap was instituted in 1951.

The first new post-war model was the Trophy, a specialized 500cc machine derived from the lightweight ISDT trials bikes. Their alloy heads and barrels came from the wartime generator units, and also

Along with the revised Speed Twin and Tiger models, the Thunderbird was launched in 1949; it featured a new headlamp nacelle which also incorporated the instruments and switchgear. The 650cc Thunderbird could better 100mph (160kph), and attained icon status when it was ridden by Marlon Brando in the movie The Wild One.

fitted on the production Grand Prix models. The official British team got through the 1948 International Trophy without penalty, and the resulting productionized model was named the Trophy in celebration. Today these lean machines are highly prized classics.

Next came the 6T or Thunderbird, launched in 1949, which was the first model to benefit from the modern styling. Apart from a larger bore and stroke, mechanically it was not so very different from the Speed Twin, but the uprated styling and creature comforts were something to shout about. There was the duplex cradle frame, and the bigger bikes got dual seats instead of a single saddle. Both the 5T and 6T reverted to the external drain pipes running from valve wells to pushrod covers, while all models were given improved gearboxes incorporating the speedo drive. Acceleration was better, but the sprung hub rear wheel continued to cause consternation at faster speeds, due to a weaving motion set up in excess of 65mph (105kph).

To give the Thunderbird a good send-off, three production bikes were ridden from Meriden to the banked Montlhéry circuit near Paris where a team of riders – including race-tester Percy Tait – averaged 92mph (148kph) riding side by side over 500 miles (800km). Such a stunt had never been pulled off before, and the bikes were ridden back to the factory, cleaned up and sent straight to Earl's Court for the bike show. The Thunderbird was quickly seized on as the bike to have, thanks to Marlon Brando's rebel posturing with one in the 1954 movie *The Wild One*. With a name derived from Red Indian mythology, it just had to sell well in the States.

Thus the Thunderbird was on its way, and its sporting version, the Tiger 110, came out in 1954. The number '110' was meant to indicate its potential top speed, although in fact it was capable of nearly 120mph (193kph). Using the new pivoted fork rear suspension, its specification included high compression pistons, special camshaft and meatier crank, but it retained the cast-iron head and block. Performance was more than adequate given its bigger single Amal Monobloc carburettor; the first twin-carb heads appeared in 1955, and were known as delta heads.

The 350cc 3T *de luxe* model was dropped at this point, mainly because its production was at variance with the larger models, and it was less popular than the 5T and 6T. On these two, a rectangular pilot light was mounted under the headlight, and there was a switch from Amal to SU carbs at this time, too.

RISING OUTPUT

In spite of the difficulties of post-war component supply – when certain items and materials were unavailable, and it was impossible to renew machine tools – production at Meriden had risen from an output of 9,477 units in 1947 to 14,306 by 1951, more than half of which were exported. Of these, some 1,000 bikes went to California. It was clear to Edward Turner that there was equal sales potential in the Eastern states, and the Triumph Corporation was set up at Baltimore in 1951 as a wholly-owned subsidiary, with ex-patriot Englishman Denis McCormack as president, supported by a team of experienced bike people. Bill Johnson was understandably less than happy about this intrusion into 'his' territory, but in the years to come the Triumph Corporation easily outsold Johnson Motors Inc. by a consistent margin of 1,000 machines; for example in 1960, the California agent sold 2,787 units to Baltimore's 3,799. There was a certain amount of opposition from Harley Davidson, who resented the outside intrusion and persuaded its East Coast dealers not to handle Triumphs, but McCormack found it relatively easy to recruit ex-servicemen to form a new dedicated dealer network. Both East and West Coast operations set up training programmes to instruct personnel in Triumph sales, maintenance and business management.

BSA BUY-OUT

Back in 1939, Jack Sangster had sold Ariel to BSA, with a proviso that if he should ever want to sell off Triumph, the Birmingham firm would have first refusal. By 1951 Sangster was ten years away from retirement, but already viewing the prospect of his heirs paying death duties with realistic concern. At this point he decided to sell Triumph, and accordingly BSA paid £2,448,000, which was split 90–10 per cent between Sangster and Turner. The latter remained fully in control, however, with no interference from BSA, the new owners. The two firms would remain competitors, with unwavering marque loyalties both sides of the factory gates.

In 1956 Sangster was appointed chairman of BSA in the wake of Sir Bernard Docker's acrimonious departure, and with Turner's enrolment as chief executive of BSA Automotive Division, there were now three motorcycle manufacturers under his command, as well as the Daimler motor vehicle and Carbodies taxi concerns. The effect was inevitably to distance Turner from the day-to-day running of Triumph, and in 1961, with Sangster's retirement, Bert Hopwood yielded to pressure from Turner and returned to Meriden as general manager from his fourteen-year stint at Norton.

Turner, meanwhile, was very much alive to exactly what the opposition was up to, and foresaw increasing competition from the emerging Japanese makers. Although the size of Jap bikes was not at this stage comparable with Triumph machines – mostly up to 300cc – the quality was good, production volumes were impressive, and technically, specifications were advanced, with electric starters and trafficators on the most humble machines. Most importantly, prices were low.

Turner flew to Japan in 1960 on a mission to discover just how real was the threat in sales and production terms. He visited Honda, Yamaha and Suzuki, and was impressed by the levels of mechanization, machine tooling and the use of rolling roads for testing. While Triumph never made 1,000 units of any particular model in a week, the Japanese firms were producing these volumes in a single day. Suzuki management had already visited Meriden, and their people were equally accommodating of Turner. At Honda, Triumph machines were politely described as 'old-fashioned', and it was enough to persuade him that the traditional British export markets were anything but secure.

SMALL IS BEAUTIFUL

There is considerable mileage in marketing terms in 'getting 'em hooked while they're young', and Turner's attention focussed on the lower end of the market in the early 1950s. Accordingly, in November 1952 Triumph came out with the 149cc T15 Terrier. It was a four-speed, 150cc overhead valve sloping single, costing £125, with the now familiar Triumph nacelle styling, telescopic forks and finished in the amaranth colour scheme of the Speed Twin. Yet it was not 'youngsters' but three of the top men at the factory – Turner himself, Bob Fearon the works director and service manager

Alex Masters – who gave the Terrier its debut: their staged 1,000-mile (1,609km) economy run from Land's End to John O'Groats was dubbed the Gaffers' Gallop by *Motor Cycling* magazine, and they achieved the rather bizarre average of 108.6mpg (2.6l/100km) at 36.68mph (59kph).

Although the Terrier wasn't a particularly cheap bike, it represented the first step on the Triumph ladder for a lot of new riders. The styling and cosmetics echoed that of the bigger models, while the overhead valve, single-cylinder Triumph engine made the bike distinctive from its ubiquitous Villiers and burgeoning two-stroke-engined contemporaries. The Terrier's engine was nearly square and built in unit with the four-speed gearbox, fed by an Amal 332 carburettor. Until 1954 it was dogged by a weak big-end bearing, and the model was usurped by the 200cc T20 Tiger Cub earlier that year; the Terrier went out of production in 1956. As well as basically the same single-cylinder engine, the Cub used the same plunger frame and cycle components as the Terrier, with a dual seat as standard. Cubs were painted with shell-blue fuel tanks and mudguards and black elsewhere. They were initially fitted with high-level up-swept exhausts, reverting to the conventional system in 1955 when wider tyres and smaller diameter wheels were introduced. The downside of the Tiger Cub continued to be the big-end bearing, which was a sensitive affair vulnerable to the abuses of inconsiderate youthful riding. The oil pump was also considered to be somewhat inadequate.

Together with a number of revisions, the Cub received a new frame with pivoted fork rear suspension in 1957, with hydraulic dampers for the front forks. Alongside the standard model, a low-geared trials competition version called the T20C was available, with typical fixtures such as high-rise exhaust, simple blade-type mudguards and a crankcase shield instead of a centre stand. Both versions were now finished in silver-grey, and in 1958 they went over to Zenith carbs instead of Amal. The following year the regular T20 was clad in a skirt, which enclosed the section below the seat down to the crankcase.

For 1960, the T20C was superseded by the much more specialised and austerely specified T20S, and this too was divided into T20T and T20S/L variants in 1961. During the next couple of years, further specialized options took the competition Cub versions deeper into the somewhat overlapping off-road disciplines of trialing, scrambling and enduro events where they performed admirably; they are still favoured in classic pre-1965 trials today. In fact I have a soft spot for the Tiger Cub, as it was one of the first bikes I ever rode as a teenager. The Tiger Cub's light weight, good handling and willing engine made it a favourite among the trials fraternity, and it was ridden by the works trialing team. In 1959 they won the arduous Scottish Six Days' Trial and took the Manufacturers' Team Award and 200cc class prize using T20s. The same year, Californian Triumph dealer Bill Martin left the American Motorcycle Association's two-way record for 200cc machines at 139.82mph (224.97kph) on a Tiger Cub, hitting 149.31mph (240.23kph) on one of his runs. Some Tiger Cub! Including the swinging-arm frame of 1958, a number of variants was built over the years, and users included the French army who took delivery of T20S/H Sports Cubs in 1965.

Cosmetic changes brought two-tone finishes of red and silver-grey in 1964, but in 1966 the name was changed to Bantam Cub as the model took on the BSA frame in a corporate rationalization. Although at first the Triumph tank was retained, other details such as the headlight, toolbox and oil tank were Bantam items, and in 1967, its last year in production, the T20S/C Super Cub was given the Bantam-shaped tank as well.

The Cub story doesn't quite end there, as three BSA-built Triumph-badged derivatives appeared in the late sixties and early seventies, called the Trophy TR25W, T25SS Blazer, and TR5MX Avenger. Whatever their merits as BSA models – dubious because of their weak engines – they were commercial failures as Triumphs.

UNIT CONSTRUCTION

In car manufacturing terms, unit-construction refers to the all-in-one monocoque body shell, but unit-construction Triumphs has mechanical connotations, referring to the fabrication of the engine and gearbox. Now, the crankcase was extended to house the gear cluster in a separate compartment.

In 1957 Triumph brought out the 3TA, a 350cc twin which was also known as the Twenty-One. This was a dual reference to the company's twenty-first anniversary, as well as to the US equivalent of measuring cubic capacity in cubic inches: 350cc equalled 21 cu in. The unit-construction gearbox produced a neater package, although the basic format of the engine was the same as the regular vertical twin. It was finished to look like an alloy unit in order to match the gearbox section. For the first time, here was a production Triumph with extensive body panelling. The area below the twin saddle and the upper portion of the rear wheel was shrouded in a curved fairing, while under the side-hinged seat lurked a basic toolkit with each piece set in a moulded rubber container. The shape of the generous front mudguard tended to echo the helmet-like 'bathtub' covering around the rear wheel.

In 1959 came the new 5TA Speed Twin, finished in amaranth but otherwise virtually identical in appearance to the bathtub look of the 3TA. The first unit-construction Tiger was the T100A of 1961, which shared the enclosed look of its siblings. These were modestly powered touring machines, although by 1964 the 3TA's scooteresque cloak had been cut back to a skirt; these claddings had completely disappeared by 1966. For riders wanting sporting bikes in this capacity range, there was a succession of variations on the T100 Tiger theme, none of which was cluttered with extraneous fairings. There were consistent mechanical improvements, and by 1966 four versions of the Tiger were available, based on a new frame and forks, as well as the less powerful T90 which lasted until 1969. Models included the off-roading T100R and T100C with fancy high-rise exhaust pipes and silencers, the TR5T Trophy Trail of 1973, which was also marketed as the Adventurer: and the high-performance T100R Daytona of 1971. The Adventurer used a frame and cycle components sourced from the BSA parts bin, and sadly the bike's name promised more than it could deliver. But by this stage the Tiger range represented the most profitable end of the company's business, as the big bikes were in serious financial difficulties. Progress on the smaller machines was thus brought to a standstill, although the Tiger range continued to be produced until the acrimonious factory closure in 1973.

SCOOTER BOYS

The post-war scooter boom was really the province of the Italian makes Vespa and Lambretta, but Triumph attempted to break into the market in 1959 with the one- and two-cylinder Tigress models. Identical models came from BSA, known as the Sunbeam.

The 350cc TR5T Trophy Trail was also marketed as the Adventurer, superseding the off-road Trophy T100C in 1973. The high-rise two-into-one exhaust system finished up alongside the rear light.

The base-model Tigress TS1 was powered by an air-cooled two-stroke 172cc BSA Bantam-derived engine, while the TW2 and the TW2S used 249cc ohv twins. All three had identical bodywork, loosely based on 1950s science-fiction robot shapes, if anything rather more attractive than their Italian contemporaries. Production of the TW2 continued until 1964, and the TS1 finished a year later.

The Tigress was probably too powerful for the typical scooterist, and in 1962 Triumph launched the 100cc Tina. This machine was smaller than the Tigress, as well as the majority of scooters around at

the time, and it had automatic transmission, possibly to tempt the female rider. Although technically quite interesting, it proved unreliable in practice.

To an extent, Triumph's scooters were on a hiding to nothing, branded with the stigma of their rocker-riding siblings as far as the scooter-obsessed Mod culture was concerned. This burgeoning early-sixties market ridiculed anything which had not emerged from the factories of Piaggio or Innocenti, and with blinkered hostility vilified the Tigress because of its motorcycle ancestry. The unfortunate Tina was treated with derision by Mod scooterists who, if they

Edward Turner recognized the need for small commuter machines, and in 1962 Triumph introduced the Tina scooter, notable for its automatic transmission. However, it was underdeveloped when launched, and too late to catch the volume scooter market.

even bothered to notice it, were oblivious of its origins. As far as the classic bike and scooter market is concerned today, the situation has not changed. Far better to pass on quickly to what Triumph was best at.

ENTER THE BONNEVILLE

Attempts to break speed records were much more common pre-war and in the 1950s than they are today. Now, the frontiers of outright speed on land and water have been pushed back to such an extent that only jet-powered vehicles need apply. But in 1955 a specially built 650cc Triumph engine powered Texan Johnny Allen's 14ft- (4m-) long 'Cigar' to 193mph (310kph) on the Bonneville salt flats in Utah. Rivalry with NSU saw the Germans raise the record to 211mph (339kph) in 1956, and Allen retaking the honours with an amazing 214mph (344kph). However, the sport's governing body, the *Fédération Internationale Motocycliste*, refused to acknowledge the US achievement because no FIM judge was present, and this provoked hostility with Meriden. Matters were put to rights when a

Triumph-powered streamliner returned to Bonneville in 1962, and Bill Johnson – not the Pasadena distributor – set the record at 224.57mph (361.33kph).

As far as the Americans were concerned there was no controversy, and the attendant publicity was excellent for Triumph. Despite the bleakness of the salt flats where the record breaking was carried out, there was much magic in the place-name 'Bonneville', so when they needed a name for the powerful new twin-carb 650 they were developing, 'Bonneville' was an obvious choice; it appealed to US buyers, of course, and also paid tribute to Johnny Allen's record-breaking exploits. A motorcycle legend was in the making, and even today, Triumph fans wait with baited breath for a new Bonneville to emerge from the Hinckley factory.

Although the Bonneville was launched at the 1959 Earl's Court Show, it had been a long time coming. While Meriden's development engineers had been occupied with extracting more performance from the twin carburettor 650 engine, with the very capable hands of Percy Tait wringing 128mph (205kph) out of it at the motor industry's MIRA testing ground, performance-addicted Rockers resorted to tuning their bikes using factory race-kits.

When they were sure it worked, Turner gave his blessing for production in August 1958. The Bonneville was an overnight sensation, with customers quick to maximize its performance potential. Although it was equally at home as a two-up tourer, for many years the T120 was the dominant force in the production racing category. Winners included Malcolm Uphill who won the 1969 Isle of Man Production TT at 99.99mph (160.88kph), putting up the first ever 100mph (160kph)-plus lap on the Manx course in the process. Other Bonnevilles finished high up regularly, and

Uphill and Tait shared a Bonnie to take the honours in the Thruxton 500-mile (804km) race in 1965. This spawned a special factory-tuned limited edition of the Bonneville, known as the Thruxton, which proved to be a regular winner. Producing 54bhp at 6,500rpm, it was capable of 140mph (225kph), and the options list included a fairing. The factory promotions' people described the Bonneville as 'The Best Motorcycle in the World', and it was probably at this point in the mid-sixties that the Bonnie reached the peak of its career.

BIG UNIT TWINS

There were three machines in the Triumph range to suit serious sports and touring riders and, in 1963, construction of the powertrains for the 6T Thunderbird, the TR6 Trophy and the T120 Bonneville went over to unit construction. The majority of engine internals remained as before, the significant difference being the rearward extension of the crankcase to incorporate the gearbox, like the smaller capacity machines. When it came out, the T120 'Bonnie' was fitted with the familiar headlamp nacelle, but they quickly reverted to the traditional unfaired headlight arrangement so the unit could be detached when the bike was ridden in competition.

The touring-orientated Thunderbird retained the skirting around its rear quarters until 1966, its last year in production, as well as the headlight nacelle, while the Trophy was more sparsely specified, just like the Bonneville. While the TR6 lacked the sporting T120's sometimes troublesome twin carb set-up, it was nonetheless a competent performer, renowned for reliability, economy and easy maintenance. Also in 1966, the bikes went over to 12-volt electrics, the tank badge was revised, and a small luggage rack was also fitted on all models. Stopping a Bonneville from high speed had always been on the tricky side, and the introduction of twin leading shoe front brakes in 1968 went a long way to making this process less fraught. By 1973 the Bonnie had a disc at the front.

In the late sixties, off-road versions of the Trophy and Bonneville were made for the US market, featuring high-level exhaust pipes and chunky tyres. The US-spec Bonnie – the T120TT – was a tuned-up all-out scrambles machine with no concessions whatsoever to road use. Similarly the North American version of the Trophy, the TR6C, was built as an off-roader, and there were

even different specifications for eastern and western states; for instance, over in California they liked them as raw as possible. A small batch of T120RT production racers was made to contest the US-based AMA series in 1970, using bored-out 744cc engines, and Gene Romero took the honours on one in 1970 and came second in 1971.

THE TRIDENT TRIPLE

Rumours of Honda's forthcoming CB750 prompted Bert Hopwood and Doug Hele to plan a rival as far back as 1963. Not knowing what configuration the new Honda

Triumph brought in UK design specialists Ogle to style the Trident, and by 1972 when it got five gears, the T150V's 'ray-gun' silencers had been replaced by conventional megaphone cans, while parts-bin slim-line forks and conical hubs replaced 1968 originals. A front disc replaced inadequate twin leading shoes in 1973.

engine might take, they came up with a triple which they called the 'Tiger-and-a-half'. The prototype of 1965 was actually styled by the trendy British design-house Ogle (noted mainly for the Reliant Scimitar GTE), and the bike's lines were rather more elegant than contemporary Bonnevilles, which appeared bruisers by comparison. Its fuel tank was likened to a loaf of bread, and the flared silencer with its triple tail pipes came to be known as a 'Flash Gordon'; another distinctive feature was the oil cooler at the top front of the frame. The triple weighed some 40lb (18kg) more than a 650 twin, and the new engine neatly fitted the regular frame. The brakes were Bonneville-type, and not quite adequate for the heavier machine, but the engine was a success, delivering reliable 120mph (193kph) performance.

In a classic case of misjudgement, the Trident Triple was launched in September 1968, followed just a month later by Honda's cheaper, higher-spec CB750. Not only did the CB have five gears, overhead cam, front disc brake and electric start, it was also marketed very effectively all over the world. However, although the Trident was dogged by petty problems, largely stemming from the triple's adaptation from the twin-cylinder unit, plus poor castings, inconsistent component construction and sourcing – the engine was actually produced by BSA and used in slanted form in its Rocket 3 as well – it could out-perform the big Japanese machines thanks to better handling, and was just as quick in a straight line. Tridents twice won the Isle of Man 750 Formula event, and the victorious Trident at the 1970 *Bol d'Or* was awarded the nickname 'Slippery Sam' after covering all and sundry in oil. Slippery Sam went on to win the 1971 and 1972 Production TT as well.

Even so, the Trident never lived up to expectations as regards sales, although it evolved in line with its twin-cylinder siblings, gaining the five-speed box in 1972 and front disc brake in 1973. A model called the X75 Hurricane, drawing heavily on US chopper styling, appeared briefly in 1973, and used the triple engine in inclined Rocket 3 format. A fibreglass moulding clad the fuel tank and extended backwards to cover the seat frame, and the X75 featured an impressive three-megaphone exhaust arrangement on the right-hand flank.

Meanwhile in 1971 a major relaunch of the three big unit twin models saw the introduction of a brand-new frame for the Trophy TR6R, the TR6C and the Bonneville TR120R. It was not altogether successful, however: the enlarged top and seat tubes of the new frame acted as the oil tank, which had the undesirable effect of raising the height of the seat and thus the centre of gravity; there were new slender forks and conical hubs, but the effectiveness of the front brakes was compromised by too-short levers; and the newly introduced flashing indicators also proved to be unreliable. Cosmetic changes included new side panels, and megaphone-style silencers, which in the case of the TR6C were strikingly mounted as a pair high up on the left-hand side of the bike.

The Bonneville was upgraded to the T140 in 1973 when it received a new engine, initially of 725cc, later rising to 744cc like the American T120RT racer, and there were also major revisions to the cylinder head. There was now a five-speed gearbox for all models – with a 'V' in the name to distinguish the fact, as in T140V – while the existing cycle parts and running gear of the old T120 were retained. By now though, the big, relatively sophisticated four-pot Japanese machines such as the Honda CB750, the Suzuki GT750 and the 903cc Kawasaki Z1 were re-writing the script, and the Bonnie was hard pressed to keep up with the plot; the Triumph rider on his enlarged and superannuated parallel twin was subjected to almost unbearable vibration levels. The message was clear by now, and the Trophy and four-speed Bonnevilles were axed at the end of 1972. A year later, the company collapsed.

Throughout 1973, efforts were made to shore up the ailing BSA/Triumph group, with a possible subsidy coming from the Department of Trade and Industry. Meanwhile in July 1973, Triumph was conscripted into BSA's merger with the Norton-Villiers group to form NVT. Norton-Villiers' origins lay in the defunct Associated Motor Cycles corporation which went down in 1966, having encompassed a number of famous names including Matchless, AJS, Norton, James and Francis Barnett. It was now the intention that the Meriden factory would close down and that production of Triumph's remaining models – the T100R, TR5T, T120V and the T140V – would take place at the BSA works at Small Heath, Birmingham. Ironically, Edward Turner, the man who had built Triumph into the formidable company it was during the fifties and sixties, died in August 1973 without witnessing the ensuing mayhem.

THE SIT-IN

The Triumph workforce was justifiably furious about the prospect of sackings and the takeover of its products and, instead of a shut-down, the gates of Meriden were locked from the inside in September 1973, and a hard-nosed, eighteen-month-long sit-in ensued. Whether this could happen today is a moot point. In the early 1970s, the unionized working class was still flexing its muscles in the coal pits, railways and motor industry, while libertarian views that we take rather for granted now, had to

an extent yet to emerge from the campuses. Thanks to sweeping changes which came about in the 1960s, the social climate of the early 1970s was still volatile, and sit-ins and demonstrations continued to be in vogue, particularly about issues such as the Vietnam war. Against this background, a dedicated and highly motivated workforce which suddenly saw itself about to be unceremoniously dumped, took matters into its own hands and revolted.

The broadly upper middle-class Conservative government of Edward Heath succumbed to the miners' strike of 1972, ushering in Harold Wilson's ostensibly working class Labour regime for the second time. This allowed idealist Tony Benn to experiment with the socialist concept of the workers' co-operative, and as negotiations dragged on through 1974, the prospect of Meriden Motorcycles became a reality. In March 1975 the government stumped up a £4.2m loan and the gates opened once again.

During the sit-in, only a trickle of machines had left the factory, mostly T120Vs; the majority of Bonnevilles produced then were only delivered in the final months, between March and May 1975.

But if things were bad for the Triumph workforce in 1973, they were equally dire for BSA, which under NVT control ceased making its own models and produced only the T150V and later the T160V Triumph Trident. With disc rear brake, left-hand side gear shift and electric start now, these were popular with police forces, and the T160V lingered on until 1977 when Wolverhampton-based NVT itself toppled. However, the Trident colours were taken up again by former Meriden race shop manager Les Williams, who built fine, customized replicas of the celebrated *Bol d'Or*-winning Slippery Sam racer, known as T160V Legends, and which continued into the mid-1980s.

THE MERIDEN CO-OP

Several co-operatives sprang up under Tony Benn's guidance in 1975, but Triumph was the most enduring. The main problem was that of cash flow, largely because motorcycles are bought in spring and summer, and winter in particular is a fallow period. With each successive year there was a financial crisis, and the workforce had to be regularly pruned. The US market, for so long courted by UK manufacturers, now posed technical difficulties thanks to the Environmental Protection Agency which demanded performance-stifling emissions controls. Both Meriden's new 1976-spec models, the TR7V Tiger and T140V Bonneville, had to undergo convoluted testing to satisfy the US legislation. These machines shared the familiar 744cc engine, with two carbs on the Bonneville and one for the Tiger, while the gear-shift was relocated on the left and a rear disc brake now fitted. A cosmetic addition to the range

arrived in 1977 to mark the Queen's Silver Jubilee, suitably liveried in red, white and blue. Just 2,400 of these special Bonnevilles were made, with strict allocations for US and UK markets. In this year too, a further £1m was fed to Triumph, by courtesy of GEC under the auspices of Lord Weinstock.

An upgraded model was introduced for the States in 1978, the T140E, featuring a new head and different carburation to cope better with the emissions decrees. This model replaced the T140V on the domestic market in 1979, when both it and the Tiger went over to electronic ignition. The T140ES was equipped with electric start – standard issue from 1981 – and the Executive model which appeared in 1980 came with a Sabre faring plus Sigma panniers and top-box. Cast-alloy Morris wheels replaced Lesters, while a chopper prototype called the Phoenix was demonstrated at the 1981 Earl's Court show.

There was excellent news for Meriden late in 1981, when the Labour government wiped out the co-op's debt. This enabled

From 1975 to 1983, the 744cc Bonneville was built by the Meriden co-operative, and in 1976 the gear shift was moved over to the left-hand side. This 1978 T140E model belonging to photographer Simon Clay has high bars and rear disc brake, plus modified head and revised carburation to suit US emission controls.

Triumph to become a limited company, with directors and the workforce becoming the shareholders. Confidence thus boosted, a new model was launched at the Paris show, the TR7T Tiger Trail. It still relied on the old frame and 744cc power unit, but it looked the part with high-rise exhaust system and knobbly tyres. The bottom end of the market was catered for by the re-introduction of the Thunderbird, powered by the single carb short-stroke 649cc motor and fitted with drum brake at the rear. In 1981 there would be a 649cc version of the Tiger Trail.

Another limited-edition special coincided with the Prince of Wales' marriage to Lady Diana Spencer. Known as the T140 Royal, it came with alloy wheels and Bing carburettors instead of the ubiquitous Amals. There was no shortage of innovation and creativity at Meriden, and the fruits of rubberized anti-vibration engine mounting trials were about to be manifested in Bonnevilles for the police, and productionized along with an all-alloy eight-valve engine with twin Amals. The new power unit was launched in 1982, powering the handsome T140TSS Bonneville. Another all-new water-cooled eight-valve twin with chain-driven overhead cams was announced in early 1983, the engine – code-named Diana – acting as a stressed member of the frame, with monoshock rear suspension and the by-now obligatory alloy wheels, disc brakes and telescopic front forks. The machine was known as the Phoenix 900.

A pair of short-stroke 599cc Thunderbird and Daytona models were introduced at the same time, but this proved to be the co-op's final shot: in spite of its upbeat attitude, not enough people bought the bikes. This was as much to do with the fact that for the mass of the population, cars were in fashion and bikes were not, rather than any inadequacy in Triumph's products. By mid-1983 the money had run out, and it was time to call in the liquidators. Towards the end of the year the plant and machine tools were auctioned off. The buyer, of the Triumph name at any rate, was a businessman and property tycoon called John Bloor.

THE DEVON CONNECTION

From a PR point of view it made sense to keep the flag flying, and John Bloor granted a franchise to Les Harris of Racing Spares to build Bonnevilles for the next five years from a factory at Newton Abbot in Devon. Harris had been producing motorcycle spares himself for some twenty years, and was well placed to continue the production process. The frame and cycle parts were much as before, although the engine components were made on new CNC lathes for greater accuracy. But with the demise of the British motorcycle industry, the supporting parts network had sunk, too. Using a variety of component sources, including Italian Paioli forks, Brembo brakes and Veglia instruments, Harris-built Bonnevilles started appearing in 1985. There were some economies, such as a reversion to kick-starters, and older Amal carbs were fitted. However, these only served to accentuate the bike's old-fashioned appearance. Although two specifications of the bike were built – one for the UK and one for the US market – the company elected to drop the North American version because of the potentially bankrupting costs of US product liability claims. To insure against such eventualities was far too costly for the operation as it was then.

By 1988, Harris's license to build Bonnevilles had expired, but not before he applied the revered Matchless name to a single-cylinder 500cc Rotax rotary-engined machine. Meanwhile, John Bloor had been creating the new Triumph plant at Hinckley.

3 The Renaissance of Triumph

After John Bloor bought the remains of the Meriden co-operative in 1983, little was known publicly of his plans for the company's future. Mr Bloor's own building company constructed the new factory on a ten-acre (4ha) green-field site, situated on Jacknell Road in the Dodwell's Bridge industrial estate, just off the busy A5 trunk road on the outskirts of Hinckley.

As factory sites go, it is ideally located, near to the M6 and M42 motorways, and a stone's throw from some attractive Leicestershire countryside, yet close to the urban facilities and supermarkets of Hinckley. The plant itself is compact too, a series of single-storey, aircraft-hanger sized buildings and corrugated roofs with extractor funnels protruding. These are the production and despatch areas. A modern, smoked-glass facade conceals a two-storey office and administration block with reception, canteen and meeting rooms on the ground floor. This is the most prominent part of the factory, although it is in fact a rather small proportion of the plant as a whole. Outside is a neat shrubbery with lots of low, ground-hugging evergreens interspersed with cherry trees, which seems quite appropriate for a forward-looking organization.

The company's 'future' is less than a mile away, where they already have the site for another brand-new factory. The signposts on

Before production started at the Hinckley plant, Triumph produced a number of prototypes to show to potential dealers. One was this Daytona 1000, finished in two-tone blue and white.

the access road are in position for it even now, although at the time of writing not a breeze-block had been laid. Noticing one of these signs in mid-1996, I drove up the access road, expecting it to be a short cut to the existing factory, but it petered out in a field. Likely to be operational by the turn of the century, the new plant will occupy a 42-acre (17ha) site, and it is intended to take capacity up to 25,000 bikes a year. Naturally there will be a transitional phase when any teething problems can be ironed out. During this period production is likely to be split 60–40 with the existing factory, with eighty bikes a day being the initial objective. The present plant has been continuously stream-lined, with countless minor adjustments made to the line, plus impressive major innovations such as the chroming plant and paint shop in the company's move towards self-sufficiency, and this is probably the way the new factory will evolve.

The renaissance of Triumph was not pro-claimed with a fanfare of trumpets, which is a rather appealing aspect of the modest Mr Bloor's character. Indeed, the nature of the new line was somewhat shrouded in mys-tery, and the first tangible indications of new machines was at a convention in the United States in 1988 where some engine castings were exhibited. However, it was not until September 1990 that the world had the chance to see the new Triumphs, when the bikes were launched at the Cologne Show with the range-topping Tro-phy 1200. A number of variations on colour schemes were shown to dealers to whet their appetites, some of which failed to make it to the production line. But by April 1991 the first of the new models were appearing in the showrooms, and by Sep-tember 1991 the whole introductory range was in place. Although production was painfully slow at first, at just eight bikes a day on average, by 1996 a new machine was

rolling off the line every six minutes, with annual production totalling 15,000 bikes. They were now on a par with Ducati.

Even so, in 1997 it seemed unlikely that John Bloor aspired to match BMW's 55,000 or Harley-Davidson's 110,000 volumes, although potentially 50,000 bikes a year might be achievable, if not necessarily desir-able, in the new factory. In company terms, Mr Bloor preferred to keep Triumph small and therefore more adaptable, able to react swiftly to changes in the market and cus-tomer preference. It is equally likely that Triumph will contest other niches where it is not currently a player, and as new models appear, we may yet see the revival of famous model names such as the Bonneville. Most of the others have already been re-allocated.

COMPONENT SOURCING

At the outset, all six bikes shared many com-mon features, including chassis, fuel tanks, engine components and running gear, and it was – and still is – quite remarkable how much of the complete bikes were made and fettled in house. It was clear that the new regime had started with a clean slate, as there was nothing on the bikes from the old days. While plans were being laid for the new range, Triumph contacted previous sup-pliers to see if they were prepared to get involved – firms such as Amal carburettors, for example; apparently they are still wait-ing for a reply. On the other hand, Kayaba suspension technicians travelled all the way to Hinckley to assist with fine-tuning the frame and suspension systems. While all Triumph models used basically the same frame, minor differences (10mm) in wheel-base were accounted for by different length forks and suspension angles.

When sceptics – and enthusiasts – looked for influences for the new machines, the

The unfaired Trident was launched in 1991 as a 750 and 900 machine, and in its quiet, unassuming way it provides the backbone of the range.

best they could come up with as a precedent was the Kawasaki GPz 900, mainly because it had a traditional diamond-pattern frame and the Triumph motor bore similarities with the Kawasaki unit. In fact Triumph engineers had ample opportunity to study every significant machine on the market before deciding which way to go with the fresh product. With the engine, for instance, there were clear advantages in having cams driven by an end-of-camshaft chain, because placing it there allowed cylinders to be positioned closer together, rather than having a camchain tunnel running through the middle of the engine. The result was a much more compact engine unit. In fact they were given much free help and advice on sources and processes by most of the Japanese firms as well as Harley Davidson during the interim years. Once they went into production though, Triumph were on their own.

When Triumph relaunched in 1991, the infrastructure once abundant in the British motorcycle industry to support them was no longer in evidence, and Japan was the obvious source for critical items such as brakes and suspension. By 1996, Japanese content in Triumphs still amounted to 19 per cent in line items, about the same as Harley Davidson's, in fact, with Triumph's own contribution at around 65 per cent of the bike; in Japanese makes such as Honda and Yamaha the figure for in-house manufactured components is around 30 per cent. This is because the Japanese parts industry is on their own doorstep, and a lot of them are owned by the bike manufacturers anyway. Even ostensibly specialist firms such as damper-makers Ohlins or White Power are owned by Yamaha and Honda respectively, so for Triumph to go with specialists does not necessarily bring the sourcing of parts any closer to home. Being an international

Model: Trident 750 and 900

Style		Roadster
Engine		
Type		Liquid-cooled, DOHC, in-line three-cylinder
Capacity		749cc (900: 885cc)
Bore/stroke		76mm × 55mm (900: 76mm × 65mm)
Compression ratio		11.0:1 (900: 10.6:1)
Carburettors		Three × 36mm flat side CV
Transmission		
Primary drive		Gear
Clutch		Wet, multi-plate
Gearbox		Six-speed
Electrics		
Ignition		Digital, inductive type
Headlight		Single × 12 volt 60/55w halogen H4
Cycle Parts		
Frame		Micro-alloyed high-tensile steel
Swinging arm		Aluminium alloy with eccentric chain adjuster
Wheels	front	Alloy six-spoke, 17in × 3.5in
	rear	Alloy six-spoke, 18in × 4.5in
Tyres	front	120/70 ZR 17
	rear	160/60 ZR 18
Suspension	front	43mm forks with triple-rate springs
	rear	Monoshock, with adjustable pre-load (900: plus adjustable rebound damping)
Brakes	front	Two × 296mm floating discs, two × two-piston calipers
	rear	Single 255mm disc, single two-piston caliper
Dimensions		
Length		85in (2,152mm)
Width		29in (760mm)
Height		43in (1,090mm)
Seat height		30in (775mm)
Wheelbase		59in (1,510mm)
Weight (dry)		467lb (212kg)
Performance		
Measured to DIN 70020		
Maximum power		90bhp @ 10,000rpm (900: 98bhp @ 9,000rpm)
Maximum torque		68Nm @ 8,700rpm (900: 83Nm @ 6,500rpm)
Maximum revs		11,000rpm (900: 9,700rpm)
Colours		
1997 range		750: Quicksilver
		900: Quicksilver and Cobalt Blue, Jet Black, Ruby Red, British Racing Green and Cream
Accessories		One-, two- and three-pannier luggage systems, solo luggage, top rack, mudguard extension, fork protectors, alarm system

company, it had to go where the technology was, yet still contrive to buy in at economic levels.

By the mid-1990s, however, an increasing number of UK firms were investing in motorcycle technology, and some have found their way onto Triumphs, such as the six-piston caliper brakes and the black box engine management system. As Triumph became more involved with the accessory markets, they were able to explore the efficiency of British firms with a view to the possible manufacture of production items. A cheaper cost-base made North America an attractive supplier too, especially for items such as polycarbonates, where Europe lagged a little way behind. One key factor in US efficiency is the bogey of product liability, where the lawyers have made it vital for manufacturers to get it right, or face massive compensation damages. It is also good reason for caution on the part of exporters, and not a few manufacturers have avoided the US market because of it. To its credit, Triumph is not one of them.

HIGH-TECH SET-UP

When visiting the factory the overriding impression is of batteries of high-tech machines, lathes and jigs in lofty, spacious workshops; only the densely packed Assembly shop area is anything like a traditional production line. As we shall see, the plant was equipped with the very latest CAM and CNC equipment, from lathes to welders, and it showed in the high quality of the motorcycles. By comparison, the Japanese motorcycle plants are beginning to look quite dated, and given Triumph's clean-sheet approach, perhaps this is only to be expected. Some Japanese factories are now forty and fifty years old, and I have heard tell of holes in the skylights at a Kawasaki plant.

Labour costs in Europe are very high, and automation was the only realistic economic route Triumph could take. Production was geared up accordingly. The six models in the original line-up were the basic unfaired Trident in 750 triple and 900 triple form, the fully faired sports Daytona in 750 triple and 1000 four-cylinder format, and the fully faired touring-biased Trophy as a 900 triple and 1200 four-cylinder machine. Its low-set bars gave the Trophy a much more sporting attitude than the long-haul tourer it became subsequently. The Trophy seemed to loose its way in the years after its launch, as Triumph designers sought to distance it from the Daytona and Sprint models. In 1993 it was de-tuned from 125bhp to 108bhp, although torque was improved. As the riding position was altered with fitment of Trident-type bars and juggling with the footrests, the excellence of the original steering characteristics and ergonomics declined, until their re-emergence in the perfect touring machine late in 1995. Cosmetically, the Trophy was changed in 1993 with slate grey engine castings and frame, previously silver, and the exhaust was black chromed. Rectangular mirrors replaced round ones, and a digital clock appeared in the instrument panel. There were a number of revisions in 1994, including fitting four-piston caliper brakes to the 1200 Trophy. The 900 Trophy got these the following year. Three-spoke alloy wheels replaced the six-spokers, and the rear rim dropped from 18in to 17in diameter, allowing it to wear a 180-section tyre.

Maintaining the Triumph code numbering system, the Hinckley triples are coded T300s, the fours T400s. A 750 triple is a T375, and a 900 triple is a T309, while the 1997-model Daytona and Speed Triple are 5-series bikes; they are coded T595 and T509 respectively.

All models go down the line in a mixture of models rather than in batches of all of a kind, so you might see a home-market Sprint followed by an export Thunderbird or a Tiger. This does not happen on the Suzuki or Honda production lines: the Japanese build exactly the number of units of a particular model which they expect to sell in the forthcoming year, and once that quantity has been reached, they retool and build another model. Triumph's approach is more flexible, and production can be altered on a month-by-month basis according to fluctuations in the market.

Triumph's development team are housed in a long grey building on the far side of the plant car park, and the company is understandably reticent about allowing access either to the premises or to interview its staff there. The 'enthusiasts' who work in R & D are also responsible for testing the bikes under the most arduous conditions all over Europe. In the UK they use the wide expanses of Bruntingthorpe airfield in Leicestershire, and the nearby MIRA test complex in Warwickshire, which includes a delightful undulating road section and the long, daunting banked oval. Here you can go absolutely flat out for just as long as you want.

There is considerable pressure on the designers, who are entrusted with getting their calculations right so that costly alterations don't have to be made in the factory. On the design front, Triumph's R & D people initially shared CAD equipment with the Rover Group, because of the high cost of installing such sophisticated apparatus. Now, however, the Hinckley design department is graced by a bank of computers. Such facilities are essential, if not quite commonplace, allowing technicians to evolve trick chassis frames and suspension systems, with the ability to design and run an engine within a computer programme without ever having to go into metal. In simulated running, the computer will show up potential faults and assess lubrication or cooling requirements over extended periods. The CAD equipment will also produce scale models. A CAD drawing is fed into the machine, which reproduces it by laser technology as a plastic model. The Thunderbird was the first Triumph to be designed in this manner, as were the very latest T595 Daytona and T509 Speed Triple. Ninety per cent of Triumph's design work is done in house, while advice on detail areas may be sought from specialist consultants such as Lotus Engineering, Cosworth or Ricardo.

It was necessary for Triumph to take the high-tech route simply because the tolerances required today were just not attainable with old-style manufacturing techniques. They were at an advantage here, being privately owned, because there was no immediate requirement to show a return on assets involved in the business. Public companies are at the mercy of shareholders without the same vision as the manufacturer. By installing its own CAD machines Triumph became instantly more flexible without having to assemble and sub-contract, as it would if it had been a public company.

Triumph has been profitable since October 1994, when the fifty-bikes-a-day milepost was passed. However, it may be a further ten years before Mr Bloor sees a true return on his original £80m investment – happily his other interests net him a considerable £12m profit, so he can afford to be fairly relaxed about Triumph's growth and development. There is very little likelihood of Triumph ever going public, though. Mr Bloor even dismissed the idea of Triumph taking a controlling interest in another company, such as Ducati, or even reviving a charismatic but long-defunct marque's name, such as Vincent. He simply preferred to concentrate efforts on manufacturing Triumph-named bikes in Hinckley.

At fifty-three, John Bloor maintains a lively interest in Triumph, and is on site at least once every day – even when he is supposed to be on holiday, so I was told. It is he who gives the final authorization as to whether a bike goes into production or not. The hierarchy is such that there is only one other director at Triumph; responsibilities are passed down via managers to section heads, to team leaders. The general manager Karl Wharton occupies the biggest desk in the large open plan office in the first floor suite – although there is allegedly no particular significance to this.

Mr Bloor sees the new 1997 models as an evolution in his overall company strategy, based on the fact that the biggest growth in Triumph's market share over the past few years has been in the sports sector. While the previous range would undoubtedly be updated with cosmetic variations, there could be no compromise with the sporting T595 and T509. Increased production levels also made it possible to envisage individual models for other single market segments.

QUALITY CONTROL

On a tour of the factory, the visitor is constantly reminded of the company's attention to quality control, with checks made at frequent intervals, bordering on the obsessive. Apart from a few teething problems early on, there appear to have been no major setbacks during the renaissance. Perhaps the biggest, or the most publicized upset in Triumph's recent history was when a rider called Philip Peverley had a rear brake caliper smash into the rear swinging arm as a retaining bolt for the rear brake anchor arm came adrift while he was going down the M3 motorway. He had a lucky escape indeed, and the factory wisely recalled all Tridents, Sprints and Tigers for a check-up.

In some cases, early bikes were known to suffer from electrical problems, such as wiring looms collapsing, batteries swelling or burning out, and haphazard behaviour of instruments and lights; and perished or blown fork seals at under 10,000 miles (16,000km) was another criticism, along with the occasional broken speedo cable, failed oil pressure switch and leaking front master cylinder. Components prone to corrosion on earlier models were footrests and banjo unions on the brake hoses and front wheel hub. All these problems have been ironed out now by rigorous attention to detail and frequent quality checks.

EARLY SPEC

At first the company could only be reactive, in order to find out what they should build so as to be certain of success in the marketplace. They listened to what customers and dealers had to say with regard to specifications, ergonomics and colour schemes, and responded accordingly. Initially it was vital to get the production process up and running as quickly as possible, improving quality all the while.

Throughout the range, the engines were modular in concept, of distinctive appearance, and located transversely and inclined slightly forward in the frame. There were initially four engine sizes – 750, 900, 1000, and 1200 – with identical 76mm bores and varying stroke. The two triples were 55mm and 65mm stroke, giving 748cc and 885cc, and with the fourth cylinder added they became 998cc and 1,179cc. With this range, Triumph could cover several different market niches, producing everything on the same line with only minimal additional cost. The wonderful-sounding three-cylinder triple is more abundant than the more guttural four, and both configurations are water-cooled twin-cams in the modern manner. There was a horizontal joint in the crankcase, and the top section of the 'casting was combined with the wet-linered block, while a one-piece cylinder head contained a pair of cams acting on bucket and shim lifters. There were four valves per cylinder set at 39 degrees. The cams were chain-driven from the right-hand end of the crank via a tunnel in the casting, and the chain could be serviced without having to remove the head. The electronic ignition was triggered from the right-hand end of the crank, while the oil-filter cartridge was accessed underneath the crankcase. The one-piece crank was allied to vibration-damping balance shafts, the triple having one ahead of the crankshaft and the four having two. There was a sophisticated crankcase breather system to reduce pressure and minimize oil leakage, as well as to control emissions. Compression ratios were 11:1 for the short-stroke engines and 10.6:1 for the long-stroke pair. The four units used a single 36mm Mikuni carburettor, in the absence of a suitable British carb, and they could all tolerate unleaded fuel. Power output was 98bhp at 9,000rpm, red-lined at 9,700rpm.

Behind the block and above the gearbox were mounted the starter motor and generator. The six-speed gearbox was in-unit with the engine, and final drive was taken by chain on the left-hand side of the bike. Eccentric chain adjusters were built into the rear fork's wheel spindle ends. The engine was a stressed member, and was hung from the spine of the tubular frame.

Up front were Kayaba 43mm telescopic forks, and at the rising-rate rear-end a single Kayaba monoshock damper. This was adjustable remotely for pre-load settings, and while there was no way of altering compression, it did provide a four-position rebound adjuster. The initial production models used three-spoke cast-alloy wheels, and the whole package was retarded by Nissin disc brakes with twin 296mm discs and two-piston calipers at the front on Trident and Trophy, and twin 310mm floating discs and four-piston calipers on the Daytona. A single 255mm disc was common to

Although the off-roading enduro segment is not as popular in the UK as it is on the continent, Triumph went ahead with the Tiger in 1993. Their confidence was not misplaced, as it sells well in overseas markets.

Model: Tiger

Style   Enduro sports tourer

Engine
Type   Liquid-cooled, DOHC, in-line three-cylinder
Capacity   885cc
Bore/stroke   76mm × 65mm
Compression ratio   10.6:1
Carburettors   Three × 36mm flat side CV

Transmission
Primary drive   Gear
Clutch   Wet, multi-plate
Gearbox   Six-speed

Electrics
Ignition   Digital, inductive type
Headlight   Two × 12 volt 60/55w halogen H4

Cycle Parts
Frame   Micro-alloyed high-tensile steel
Swinging arm   Aluminium alloy with eccentric chain adjuster
Wheels   front   Alloy 36-spoke, alloy rim, 19in × 2.5in
                rear   Alloy 40-spoke, alloy rim, 17in × 3.0in
Tyres   front   110/80 × 19
                rear   140/80 × 17
Suspension   front   43mm forks
                rear   Monoshock, with remote reservoir, adjustable pre-load, compression and rebound damping
Brakes   front   Two × 276mm floating discs, two × two-piston calipers
                rear   Single 255mm disc, single two-piston caliper
Fuel tank   5gals 2pts (24 litres) capacity

Dimensions
Length   86in (2,175mm)
Width   34in (860mm)
Height   53in (1,345mm)
Seat height   33in (850mm)
Wheelbase   61in (1,560)
Weight (dry)   461lb (209kg)

Performance
Measured to DIN 70020
Maximum power   85bhp @ 8,000rpm
Maximum torque   82Nm @ 6,000rpm
Maximum revs   8,750rpm

Colours
1997 range   Chilli-pepper Red, Khaki Green, Jet Black, Caspian Blue

Accessories   Two- and three-pannier luggage systems, solo luggage, top rack, heavy-duty front fork springs, mudguard extension, centre stand, alarm system

all models, with the Daytona's caliper and torque arm located under the rear fork, as opposed to on top of it. The overall impression was one of quality and careful construction, and the road testers applauded the smooth, low-down torque, ample performance with reasonable economy, good stopping power and predictable handling.

It was soon clear that the 900 triple was the best seller, in Trophy form, with the Trident next best, and the Daytona accounting for only a low 10 per cent. Perhaps its styling was not sufficiently 'race-rep' for some buyers;

whatever the reason, its specification was made more attractive for power freaks with the introduction of a 1200 version in the autumn of 1992, which came with optional single seat hump and lower screen, while the 750 model was dropped. The Trophy models were also facelifted at this point, getting higher-set touring handlebars and black exhausts instead of just chrome ones. It was a sound specification for a touring bike. The Tory Roads Minister, Kenneth Carlisle, remarked at the 1992 NEC Bike Show, that the new 147bhp 1200 Daytona was so powerful that it

Launched in October 1992, the Sprint provided a halfway house between its unfaired sister, the Trident, and the fully faired Daytona and Trident models. This is a 1996 bike, with plain exhausts rather than the chromium-plated cans fitted to earlier machines.

Model: Sprint

Style   Sports tourer

Engine
Type   Liquid-cooled, DOHC, in-line three-cylinder
Capacity   885cc
Bore/stroke   76mm × 65mm
Compression ratio   10.6:1
Carburettors   Three × 36mm flat side CV

Transmission
Primary drive   Gear
Clutch   Wet, multi-plate
Gearbox   Six-speed

Electrics
Ignition   Digital, inductive type
Headlight   Two × 12 volt 60/55w halogen H4

Cycle Parts

Frame		Micro-alloyed high-tensile steel
Swinging arm		Aluminium alloy with eccentric chain adjuster
Wheels	front	Alloy three-spoke, 17in × 3.5in
	rear	Alloy three-spoke, 17in × 5.5in
Tyres	front	120/70 ZR 17
	rear	170/60 ZR 17
Suspension	front	43mm forks with dual-rate springs
	rear	Monoshock, with adjustable pre-load and rebound damping
Brakes	front	Two × 310mm floating discs, two × four-piston calipers
	rear	Single 255mm disc, single two-piston caliper
Fuel tank		5gals 3pts (25 litres) capacity

Dimensions
Length   85in (2,152mm)
Width   29in (760mm)
Height   53in (1,350mm)
Seat height   31in (790mm)
Wheelbase   58in (1,490mm)
Weight (dry)   474lb (215kg)

Performance
Measured to DIN 70020
Maximum power   98bhp @ 9,000rpm
Maximum torque   83Nm @ 6,500rpm
Maximum revs   9,700rpm

Colours
1997 range   Candy Apple Red, Nightshade, British Racing Green

Accessories   Pannier inner bags, one-, two- and three-pannier luggage systems, solo luggage, top rack, tinted high screen, mudguard extension, fork protectors, alarm system

had 'no place on the roads'. However, in the run-up to the 1997 General Election, Labour's more enlightened Tony Blair and Glenda Jackson were both seen astride new Triumphs at the Alexandra Palace Show.

The author gets acquainted with a 1996 Trophy. The bike's twin headlights give a good spread on dip, and reach out a quarter-of-a-mile ahead on main beam.

THE RANGE EXPANDS

More significantly, another name from the firm's illustrious past was revived in October 1992 with the introduction of the Tiger 900 at the Cologne Show. It was styled as a Supermoto enduro machine with *avant-garde* graphics on its tall tank and fairing. The tank was made of plastic which required homologation in the UK, and it was the first new-style tank in the Triumph range. Along with the upswept three-into-two exhausts there was a parcel rack, handlebar lever protectors and longer seat. The Tiger was constructed on a strengthened frame with an extended wheelbase, and it used wire-spoke wheels as opposed to cast alloys. To fit the stance of an off-road machine it had longer front forks, and a guard frame around the engine – which was a de-tuned 85bhp version of the now-familiar 900 unit.

The first Hinckley-made Triumph was a four-cylinder Trophy 1200, and the firm's sports-touring bike became the first of its range to receive a major facelift. This came in 1996, centering on the rotund John Mockett-designed fairings and matching Givi luggage.

Model: Trophy 900 and 1200

Style

Sports tourer

Engine

Type	Liquid-cooled, DOHC, in-line three-cylinder
Capacity	885cc (1,200: 1,180cc)
Bore/stroke	76mm × 65mm
Compression ratio	10.6:1
Carburettors	Three × 36mm flat side CV (1,200: four × 36mm flat side CV)

Transmission

Primary drive	Gear
Clutch	Wet multi-plate
Gearbox	Six-speed

Electrics

Ignition	Digital, inductive type
Headlight	Two × 12 volt 60/55w halogen H4

Cycle Parts

Frame		Micro-alloyed high-tensile steel
Swinging arm		Aluminium alloy with eccentric chain adjuster
Wheels	front	Alloy three-spoke, 17in × 3.5in
	rear	Alloy three-spoke, 17in × 5.5in
Tyres	front	120/70 ZR 17
	rear	170/60 ZR 17
Suspension	front	43mm forks with dual-rate springs
	rear	Monoshock, adjustable for pre-load and rebound damping
Brakes	front	Two × 310mm floating discs, two × four-piston calipers
	rear	Single 255mm disc, single two-piston caliper with frame-mounted torque arm

Dimensions

Length	85in (2,152mm)
Width	31in (790mm)
Height	53in (1,350mm)
Seat height	31in (790mm)
Wheelbase	58in (1,490mm)
Weight (dry)	484lb (220kg) (1,200: 518lb (235kg)

Performance

Measured to DIN 70020

Maximum power	98bhp @ 9,000rpm (1,200: 108bhp @ 9,000rpm
Maximum torque	83Nm @ 6,500rpm (1,200: 104Nm @ 5,000rpm)
Maximum revs	9,700rpm

Colours

1997 range	Pacific Blue, Merlot Red, British Racing Green

Accessories

Pannier inner bags, back rest, top rack, tinted high screen, hand wind-deflector kit, mudguard extension, colour-coordinated top box, heated grips, fork protectors, alarm system

Retro-look instrument panel and controls of a Thunderbird. Because it is a two-seater, its frame weight is biased further forward than the Adventurer, below.

With its high-rise bars, plus optional screen and custom leather panniers, the 1996 Adventurer took Triumph one step further into the retro-market from the Thunderbird. Now classic buffs could ride fine-looking machines with the advantage of modern-day reliability.

Model: Adventurer

Style   Retro-cruiser

Engine
Type   Liquid-cooled, DOHC, in-line three-cylinder
Capacity   885cc
Bore/stroke   76mm × 65mm
Compression ratio   10.0:1
Carburettors   Three × 36mm flat side CV
Transmission
Primary drive   Gear
Clutch   Wet, multi-plate
Gearbox   Five-speed

Electrics
Ignition   Digital, inductive type
Headlight   Single × 12 volt 60/55w halogen H4

Cycle Parts
Frame   Micro-alloyed high-tensile steel
Swinging arm   Aluminium alloy
Wheels   front   Alloy 36-spoke, 18in × 2.5in
                    rear   Alloy 40-spoke, 16in × 3.5in
Tyres   front   110/80 × 18
                    rear   150/80 or 160/80 × 16
Suspension   front   43mm forks with triple-rate springs
                    rear   Monoshock, with adjustable pre-load
Brakes   front   Single 320mm disc
                    rear   Single 285mm disc

Dimensions
Length   85in (2,250mm)
Width   29in (860mm)
Height   51in (1,150mm)
Seat height   29in (750mm)
Wheelbase   61in (1,550mm)
Weight (dry)   484lb (220kg)

Performance
Measured to DIN 70020
Maximum power   70bhp @ 8,000rpm
Maximum torque   72Nm @ 4,800rpm
Maximum revs   8,750rpm

Colours
1997 range   Amber and Copper, Turquoise and Silver, Aubergine and Silver,
                                Heritage Gold and Ivory, Violet and Ivory

Accessories   Leather panniers, grab rail, luggage rack, sissy bar, chrome mudguard
                                rack, mudguard pad, roadster seat, highway screen, summer screen,
                                roadster screen, chrome side panels, chrome master cylinder cover kit,
                                chrome lever kit, chrome side stand, chrome chain guard, chrome
                                water-pump pipe, low handlebar kit, mudguard extension, tank
                                knee-pads, tank pad, centre stand, fork protectors, alarm system

Alongside the Tiger came the Sprint model, which was basically a Trident 900 clad with stylish side and rear panels and a neat cockpit fairing featuring Daytona-style twin round headlights. It was, in fact, a sports-tourer. Along with the Trident, the Sprint would soon get a new aluminium rear suspension unit, adjustable for pre-load and rebound damping in case the bike ever got heavily laden.

The prayers of sports-minded Sprint fans were answered in 1996 with the introduction of an exclusive 200-off limited-edition sports version, which came with low-set bars and high-rise exhaust system, as well as a wider back tyre. Although it retained the Sprint's distinctive cockpit and tail fairings, in practice it wasn't so very different from the old Daytona.

TOURIST TROPHY

In accordance with the on-going programme of revisions, the Trophy and Daytona specification and styling were also updated. The Trophy's major facelift came in September 1995 – effectively a complete redesign – with its striking new rotund bodypanels and what I like to think of as 'cool-dude Oakley-style sunglasses' headlights. The fairings were the result of wind tunnel experiments at MIRA and gave the Trophy a unique identity.

The swooping tail fairing had been seen before on the Sprint, complete with twin passenger grab handles, but the main body fairings with their oval air intakes and slatted louvres now broadened out to give cover to the Trophy's higher, wider handlebars. Even the frame, with its revised bracketry, was given a new part number, and the only part to remain compatible with the old model was the fuel tank. It was now a grand tourer *par excellence*, with 7-gallon (32-litre)

colour-coded Givi panniers, capacious enough to house a full-face helmet fitted as original equipment. Its neat instrument binnacle now included a proper clock and fuel gauge – which road testers declared with some amazement was pretty much accurate. There was now a remote headlight adjuster for use when the rear was laden down, and there were lockable cubby holes in the facia panel. Although the engines were not altered from their high torque, low horse-power set-up, the exhaust system was changed, and the rear caliper lowered from the top of the wheel to the bottom, improving the centre of gravity just a little.

BACK TO THE FUTURE

In October 1994 Triumph took the bold step of introducing its retro-styled Thunderbird. Built on a new steel-spine frame, it encapsulated the imagery of Triumph's halcyon days with its 1950s styling, chrome plating and period paint finishes, combined with high-rise handlebars and long chrome forks which cast more than a side-long glance at both the chopper and Harley dresser fraternities. A range of custom accessories was available to go the whole way in recreating the period look, while the best bit was that the Thunderbird used the proven 900 triple and its mechanicals were all new. So no reliability problems here.

The Thunderbird's popularity was such that Triumph now felt sufficiently confident to launch the stylistically similar Adventurer at the Paris Show in September 1995. The frames were virtually identical, but the new bike was designed as a single seater, making possible the delightful upswept duck-tail rear mudguard. It had the stance of a cruiser, which made it yet more extreme than the Thunderbird. The Adventurer came with even higher-rise

Model: Thunderbird

Style	Classic roadster

Engine

Type	Liquid-cooled, DOHC, in-line three-cylinder
Capacity	885cc
Bore/stroke	76mm × 65mm
Compression ratio	10.0:1
Carburettors	Three × 36mm flat side CV

Transmission

Primary drive	Gear
Clutch	Wet, multi-plate
Gearbox	Five-speed

Electrics

Ignition	Digital, inductive type
Headlight	Single × 12 volt 60/55w halogen H4

Cycle Parts

Frame		Micro-alloyed high-tensile steel
Swinging arm		Aluminium alloy
Wheels	front	Alloy 36-spoke, 18in × 2.5in
	rear	Alloy 40-spoke, 16in × 3.5in
Tyres	front	110/80 × 18
	rear	150/80 or 160/80 × 16
Suspension	front	43mm forks with triple-rate springs
	rear	Monoshock, with adjustable pre-load
Brakes	front	Single 320mm disc
	rear	Single 285mm disc

Dimensions

Length	88in (2,250mm)
Width	34in (860mm)
Height	45in (1,150mm)
Seat height	29in (750mm)
Wheelbase	61in (1,550mm)
Weight (dry)	484lb (220kg)

Performance

Measured to DIN 70020

Maximum power	70bhp @ 8,000rpm
Maximum torque	72Nm @ 4,800rpm
Maximum revs	8,700rpm

Colours

1997 range	Cardinal Red and Silver, Imperial Green and Silver, Jet Black and Silver, British Racing Green and Cream, Jet Black

Accessories

Leather panniers, grab rail, luggage rack, sissy bar, king and queen seat, highway screen, summer screen, roadster screen, two-tone front mudguards, chrome side panels, chrome lever kit, chrome side stand, chrome chain guard, chrome water-pump pipe, low handlebar kit, mudguard extension, tank knee pads, tank pad, centre stand, fork protectors, alarm system bars, megaphone exhaust, and complemented by its sixties-inspired paint scheme and tank badges, plus a generous application of chrome – all of which was calculated to make it a striking poseur.

ACCESSORIES

Accessories are very big business in the bike industry, supposedly making more money for Harley Davidson than the machines themselves. With the new 1997 models, Triumph hoped to increase its accessory sales by producing its own equipment, thereby excluding the specialists who traditionally jump on manufacturers' coat-tails with aftermarket bolt-ons and fashion goods.

For legal reasons, Triumph's licensed clothing subsidiary, set up in January 1995, comes under the 'Triple Connection' banner. It specializes in the sort of high-quality clothing and products that you would expect to be associated with the marque, many of which Triumph riders would be more than happy to wear and use. There are top-quality leathers, in all-in-one and jean and jacket styles for riders of modern as well as classic machines, also waterproof oversuits, salopettes, jackets and jeans, gloves and full-face and open-face lids. Then there are sports boots, all-weather boots and Timberland-style 'Thunderbird' boots; also the ubiquitous monogrammed sweatshirts, baseball caps and key-fobs; T-shirts depicting each Triumph model and the Speed Triple Challenge, stylish baseball-type jackets with 'Triumph' written large on the back, besides 'paddock' jackets and lighter-weight windcheaters. In addition, there are items which it would be nice to have but which have absolutely nothing at all to do with motorcycling: all-weather cigarette lighters, wallets and credit-card holders, tailored luggage, and a range of exotic-looking wrist watches, all of which feature the Triumph logo.

Triumph was obliged to adopt the somewhat contrived 'Triple Connection' name for the accessories subsidiary because a German clothing company had bought the rights to a clothing range going under the name of 'Triumph'. Similarly, when Triumph launched an owners' club for riders of Hinckley-built machines in September 1996, they came up with the equally contrived name of 'Riders' Association of Triumph', or 'RAT' for short. There was a need to establish a forum for these new customers, and also to avoid direct confrontation with the existing Triumph owners' club. Inevitably in the future there would be a certain amount of crossover between the classic fraternity and RAT supporters, but for the moment, riders of Hinckley machines could develop and maintain a camaraderie among themselves with the prospect of factory- and dealer-led trips and special events.

HOT STUFF

By 1995 the Triumph repertoire included a faster, lighter, limited-edition version of the Daytona: the Super III, a 900 with hand-finished, lightweight, Cosworth-cast cylinder head with gas-flowed ports and high-lift cams. Bringing it to a rapid halt were six-piston caliper aluminium front brakes acting on fully floating twin discs; this was superior to the regular Daytona which used just the four-piston calipers. The discs were machined from single aluminium billet and drilled for maximum efficiency. The yellow and black coachwork incorporated several carbon-fibre sections for strength and lightness, including the front mudguard and rear hugger. The massive cans were clad in Kevlar. Only 805 units were made, and the additional cost over a standard Daytona was around £5k.

Model: **Daytona Super III**

Style   Sports

Engine
Type   Liquid-cooled, DOHC, in-line three-cylinder; high-lift cam,
                         reworked head
Capacity   885cc
Bore/stroke   76mm × 65mm
Compression ratio   12.0:1
Carburettors   Three × 36mm flat side CV

Transmission
Primary Drive   Gear
Clutch   Wet, multi-plate
Gearbox   Six-speed

Electrics
Ignition   Digital, inductive type
Headlight   Two × 12 volt 60/55w halogen H4

Cycle Parts
Frame   Micro-alloyed high-tensile steel
Swinging arm   Aluminium alloy with eccentric chain adjuster
Wheels   front   Alloy three-spoke, 17in × 3.5in
                rear   Alloy three-spoke, 17in × 5.5in
Tyres   front   120/70 ZR 17 sport compound
                rear   180/55 ZR 17 sport compound
Suspension   front   43mm forks with triple-rate springs, adjustable for compression,
                         rebound damping and spring pre-load
                rear   Monoshock, with adjustable pre-load and rebound damping
Brakes   front   Two × 310mm floating discs, two × six-piston 'Triumph 6' calipers
                rear   Single 255mm disc, single two-piston caliper with frame-mounted
                         torque arm

Dimensions
Length   85in (2,152mm)
Width   27in (690mm)
Height   47in (1,185mm)
Seat height   31in (790mm)
Wheelbase   58in (1,490mm)
Weight (dry)   465lb (211kg)

Performance
Measured to DIN 70020
Maximum power   115bhp @ 9,500rpm
Maximum torque   89Nm @ 8,500rpm
Maximum revs   9,700rpm

Colours
1995 range   Racing Yellow

Accessories   Mudguard extension, fork protectors, alarm system

The Super III of 1994 was based on the Daytona 900, and featured a highly tuned engine, carbon-fibre bodywork, a pair of six-piston caliper front brakes – and a hefty price premium as a result.

Because of this hefty premium it was not an easy model to sell when new, according to Barry Lynes, managing director of the Norfolk main dealers Lings of Watton. However, demand for secondhand ones suddenly took off once production ceased, as from then on the Super III was seen as a collectable model, and values rose accordingly.

As the unfaired designer bike boom got under way, another naked retro-bruiser appeared in 1995, an out-and-out macho machine called the Speed Triple. Definitely a bike with attitude, this Rocker's rapture used the Daytona frame and minimal tail fairing, similar but not identical to the Sprint, to produce the stripped-down, ready-for-action look of the late fifties and early sixties Café Racer. The power unit was, fairly obviously, the 900 triple,

although late in 1996 a short run of 250 bikes was produced, fitted with the old 750cc motor. These delightful end-of-the-line machines looked much the same as their bigger-engined siblings, apart from the badging and their old-style six-spoke Trident wheels instead of the normal Speed Triple's three-spoke alloys. Brake hoses were in rubber rather than stainless steel like the 900, and thus slightly less efficient, while the smaller 160-section rear Michelins made for quicker steering. The 750 Speed Triple also had the added attraction of being not only more exclusive, but £1,674 cheaper than the 900. In 1995, Triumph were able to capitalize on the performance qualities of the Speed Triple by introducing a highly successful race series in the UK, known as the Speed Triple Challenge, with

Competition brings excellent publicity, and Triumph launched the Mobil One Speed Triple Challenge race series in 1995, based around its Speed Triple model. Owners were quick to customize their machines to match the racers.

rounds held at the major circuits, frequently in support of major meetings. There was a hefty £50,000 backing from the Mobil fuel company, and a host of leading national and international riders took part.

QUANTUM LEAP

By now the company was in a position to lead from the front with its manufacturing skills. The most radical new models were launched in the autumn of 1996. There had been rumours of new machines in the motorcycle press for a while, but when Simon Clay and I were visiting the factory on a photography mission in early summer 1996 we came upon Chassis 2 team leader Guy Campton busy working on a prototype. We were truly amazed for in that instant we saw clearly that here was not just the state-of-the-art, but before us was the future of British motorcycling. At the time, of course,

nobody would admit to what it was, although we later realized it was actually an unfaired T509 Speed Triple. There was no chance of us photographing it, either; all we could do was marvel, so different did it appear to be from then-current Triumphs with its curvaceous alloy frame, bug-eye light pods, sexy panelling and three-spoke wheels – and was that really oval tubing? The image which sprang to mind at this point was the exotically styled Bimota range, and in fact first impressions turned out to be not so wide of the mark, as there *are* certain similarities between the new Triumphs and the futuristic Bimota YB9 and Mantra.

Triumph is not coy about making strategic leaks to the media, and *Motor Cycle News* scooped the new models with 'spy' photos in July, two months before they were given the exclusive front-page story in late September 1996. The motorcycle press had been well aware for nine months or so that

The 1200 Daytona is an extremely powerful bike, developing 114bhp at 8,000rpm; with the launch of the new T595, old-generation Daytonas like this are a very attractive option on the secondhand market.

big news was forthcoming, and the new machines – the T595 Daytona Supersport and the T509 Speed Triple – were launched officially at Cologne at the beginning of October 1996.

The new models had been in the throes of development under the project manager Steve Steward in Triumph's R & D shop for two years, with no fewer than seven engineers working on the motor and ten on the chassis at one point. While designers draw up their ideas for new models, the engineers are looking over their shoulders to make sure that what is being proposed will actually work in practice. The approved concept is then recreated on computer, and pitted against a programme of design requirements which sort out its strengths and weaknesses; any shortcomings are then steadily worked on. The specialist-designed frame was created on a computer screen, but could only be satisfactorily evaluated as a fully finished prototype: in the course of designing the new models, the engine was first made of wood, placed in the chassis to be integrated with the styling. Eventually it was the chief tester's job to say whether it worked or not. He and the team progressed from wind tunnel to a diverse variety of climate and altitude locations, from freezing cold to 111°F (44°C), with 100 per cent humidity and at 12,000ft (3,660m), to calibrate the requirements of the fuel injection system. And if further testimony were needed, the German government's official test rider was obviously impressed: these riders carry out the tough TUV homologation tests required by their government, and must evaluate every bike aspiring to the German market, from FireBlade down. Having completed the tests on the new T595 Daytona, their man rode it back to the factory and liked it so much that he ordered one, claiming it was the best road bike he'd ever ridden.

The new bikes were a great advance on the previously worthy range, and a quantum leap specification-wise. The new Daytona's 985cc triple was lighter, and now fuel-injected. It produced 128bhp at 10,200rpm, with a massive 72.3ft.lb of torque, placing it well on terms with state-of-the-art icons such as the FireBlade and the Ducati 916. In pre-launch testing, Triumph took the new machines to the Bonneville Salt Flats, along with a FireBlade and a Ducati 916 for back-to-back comparisons, so they could be certain that they had a winner. However, demonstrating just how fast the Japanese can respond to new threats to their domain, the Honda Blackbird pre-empted the Daytona T595 by a short head, and the VTR Fire Storm vee-twin looked set to challenge Ducati's dominance in the World SuperBike series.

Design engineer Steve Steward explained that getting away from the spine frame was essential in the quest for better performance, mainly so that the air box and fuel injection would work. They would fit much better in a perimeter frame. 'Also, the new frame would demonstrate that the new T509 and T595 were dedicated sportsbikes rather than compromises between styling and performance. This was also the first time we had used aluminium welding' he said.

Formerly the province of special builders like Harris or Spondon, the new trellis-style frame is actually derived from the beam frame, allowing the engine to serve as a rigid chassis member, contrary to the FireBlade, which relies for its strength on a massive-section beam frame. There is every likelihood that future Triumphs will be based on the T595 frame. What looks right very often is right.

Said Steward:

We wanted to ensure the styling of the new bikes would look right, too. So the T595 was designed to be lower and sleeker, smaller and lighter than the competition, yet still perceived as a Triumph. Our goal was to achieve an overall weight of 200kg, and produce a bike which could sell everywhere, even in difficult markets like Switzerland and California. The basic styling was done by a team of subcontractors led by John Mockett, and constantly re-evaluated in-house. But actually the finished article differs very little from the initial renderings, and the changes we made were necessary because of difficulties in productionizing brand-new componentry, rather than using modified items derived from existing parts, which is what we normally did in the past. The colour schemes were deliberately chosen to avoid compromising the styling and the marque's integrity. We think they give it a European feel.

No Japanese race-rep decals and stripes here then. 'Once the Japanese bikes have their stickers removed, they can look very bland,' he said.

On the development of the engine, Steward had this to say:

Triumph carried out 90 per cent of the development work on the new engines in-house, resorting to outside specialist assistance only where necessary, such as with the fuel injection system which is unique to the T595.

Being a small company, we approached specialists for advice before entering any area we were unfamiliar with.

Although heavier by 29lb (13kg) than the FireBlade, the T595's sleek new aerodynamic fairings overcame the power-to-weight differential. The Daytona's frame utilizes the engine as an additional structural member, helping to keep its chassis weight down to just 22lb (10kg). In the marketplace the Daytona was priced at £9,649, only £500 dearer than the niche-market leading Fire-Blade, yet a cool £3,000 cheaper than the Ducati. Whether this would sway Italian fans from their passion was another matter.

To achieve the performance increase, Triumph's R & D people liaised with motor-racing legends Lotus Engineering at Hethel, Norfolk, whose bread-and-butter speciality is consultancy in engine and chassis development. Lotus came up with advice on combustion chamber size for optimum gas flow, manifest in the special racing-style exhaust manifold castings: the free-flow, three-into-one joint is cast from a mould rather than manufactured from sheet steel, and is therefore thinner, lighter and perfectly formed.

Since the concept was to increase power output and reduce weight, the six-year-old T300 three-cylinder engine was altered quite radically, so that really only the conrods remained unchanged. An instant weight loss was achieved by casting the triple's engine casings, clutch, cam and breather covers in magnesium. The crankshaft, balancer, gearbox and clutch were also lightened, while the gearbox sprocket cover was made in plastic polymer. Bores were lined with aluminium to reduce drag on the racing-style semi-forged aluminium pistons. Piston-ring width is reduced by 20 per cent, improving high rev control and reducing friction. The T509's triple has a 3mm shorter bore than the

Daytona, making it 70cc smaller all told, while the T595 has a larger combustion chamber. Reprofiled cams helped boost the rev ceiling to 10,700rpm.

Both bikes have a highly sophisticated fuel-injection system, superior to any other production bike, and well ahead of the field in any case, evolved in collaboration with the French company Sagem. The disparity in engine capacities is reflected in different programming of the MC2000 engine management system, but in essence it is identical for both models. The system is monitored by a 16-bit Siemens SAHC 167 microprocessor – a black box which processes three million details a second, capable of predicting gas acceleration through the inlet tract under full throttle and maintaining the correct mixture at all times. Data is fed to the processor via sensors, co-ordinating ignition and fuel injection according to a memory map. It also incorporates an idle control circuit, which copes with additional load such as when lights are switched on, by bleeding extra air into the inlet between butterflies and inlet valves in the trick throttle bodies, and thus speeding up the idle. A hand-operated choke for cold-weather starting is therefore not included in the design. The triple was also a solidly mounted, fully stressed chassis member. Both bikes have a six-speed gearbox, and the T595s are race-derived.

A single-sided swinging-arm, located on the left of the bike, also allowed the three-into-one exhaust system to be tucked in tightly on the right-hand side. Of necessity, the swing-arm had to be slightly heavier than the old one, but by compensation, the new arrangement showed off the three-spoke Brembo wheel to great effect on both models.

The Daytona and the Speed Triple became the first production bikes to be built up on an oval-section alloy frame. Its design incorporated the now-conventional twin spars, but

Model: Daytona T595

Style   Supersports

Engine
Type   Liquid-cooled, DOHC, in-line three-cylinder
Capacity   955cc
Bore/stroke   79mm × 65mm
Compression ratio   11.2:1
Induction   Electronic fuel injection, 41mm throttle body. Controlled by Sagem
                              MC2000, computerized engine management system

Transmission
Primary drive   Gear
Clutch   Wet multi-plate
Gearbox   Six-speed

Electrics
Ignition   Digital, inductive type
Headlight   Two × 12 volt 60/55w halogen H4

Cycle Parts
Frame   Aluminium alloy perimeter, oval section aluminium extrusions;
                              engine is additional structural member
Swinging arm   Aluminium alloy, single sided with eccentric chain adjuster
Wheels   front   Brembo alloy three-spoke, 17in × 3.5in
                  rear   Brembo alloy three-spoke, 17in × 6.0in
Tyres   front   120/70 ZR 17   Bridgestone Battlax BT56
                  rear   190/50 ZR 17   Bridgestone Battlax BT56
Suspension   front   45mm forks with dual-rate springs, adjustable for compression,
                              rebound damping and spring pre-load
                  rear   Monoshock, adjustable for compression, rebound damping and pre-load
Brakes
                  front   Two × 320mm floating discs, two × four-piston calipers
                  rear   Single 220mm disc, single two-piston caliper

Dimensions
Length   83in (2,115mm)
Width   28in (720mm)
Height   46in (1,170mm)
Seat height   31in (800mm)
Wheelbase   56in (1,440mm)
Weight (dry)   436lb (198kg)

Performance
Measured to DIN 70020
Maximum power   130bhp @ 10,200rpm
Maximum torque   100Nm @ 8,500rpm
Maximum revs   10,700rpm

Colours
1997 range   Strontium Yellow, Jet Black

Accessories   Integrated alarm system, carbon-fibre rear hugger, carbon-fibre front
                              mudguard, carbon-fibre-look front tank panel, tank bag, paddock stand

with the addition of two extruded tubes which ran either side of the engine. It weighed just 24lb (11kg). Suspension both front and rear comes from Showa in Japan, with fully adjustable 45mm front forks and rear shock absorber; the brakes are also Japanese, four piston caliper front and two piston rear, by Nissin, and said to outperform the six-pot calipers. Pad specification was crucial to optimum braking performance.

The three-spoke wheels Simon and I had seen on the prototype were to be standard issue, designed in-house and made by Brembo in Italy. The one on the rear is located by a central single locking nut which is both aesthetically pleasing and practical. Made of aluminium alloy, these wheels are naturally light, which helps to minimize gyroscopic forces as well as reducing the bike's unsprung weight, contributing to superior handling and steering response. They were the first bikes to be shod as standard with sticky Bridgestone BT56 Battlax tyres, which are excellent for traction and grip in high-speed cornering. The rear tyre uses 'mono spiral belt' construction, incorporating a single continuous thread of Kevlar wrapped around its inner circumference which, together with Bridgestone's 'dual- aligned compound' technology, makes for a better contact patch, as well as longevity.

The Daytona T595's 995cc engine was developed in association with Lotus Engineering, while its three-spoke wheels were designed in-house and made by Brembo. They are shod with advanced 190/50 ZR 17 Bridgestone Battlax tyres as standard.

The detailing which makes these Triumphs so impressive can be seen better on the unfaired T509 Speed Triple. Like the infaired Ducati monster, the centrepiece of the T509 is its engine, although its naked street-fighter looks are dominated by the bright alloy chassis and minimal rear panels. The bracket work for the foot controls and rear pegs, plus the neat jointing on the spars and side tubes, is simply excellent.

THE FUTURE

The modular system is fine for convenience of production and for supporting a homogenized range of bikes, and indeed the company's renaissance was based on it, but it is also a limiting factor, and Triumph will gradually steer away from this concept and focus more on specific market niches. The Thunderbird was the first step, being only 34 per cent common parts with the rest of the range, while the latest evolution of the Trophy had some twenty updates on its predecessor.

Triumph's frontline spokesman, Bruno Tagliaferri, was reluctant to discuss plans for the future. Unlike specialist car producers Morgan and TVR who provided access to development shops when I researched books on them, there was no chance of a glimpse into the future at Hinckley, no insight into what lay on the drawing board or the computer screen after the euphoria had died down over the T595 and the T509. On every other matter, Triumph was entirely co-operative. Suffice to conjecture that since the company so carefully pinpointed and attacked the sports market with such devastating commitment, we can be sure that future incursions into specialist niches will be carried out with similar verve and style.

As Bruno says, quite revealingly I think:

The new models – the T595 and the T509 – take Triumph onto a new level; they raise our credentials in a cutting-edge sector of the market. This is the most discerning area of the market that we've gone into, and the fact that we've had a fair go at it should leave people wondering what we might go into next. Hopefully they will realize that if we can crack this one, we can crack all of them. But we won't talk about what hasn't come out yet, because we'd be shooting ourselves in the foot then.

So for the moment, we have to be content with what we can lust after in the showroom. Spending time at the factory confirms that the company is supremely buoyant, and there are more surprises in the pipeline. It is a fair bet that Triumph has its eye on the 600cc sports hot-house, traditionally the ultra-competitive and cutting-edge battleground of the CBR, ZZR, GSX and the FZR brigade. If they do enter that particular fray, they have to get it right first time – but clearly, since the T595 is such a stunning machine, the capability is there. Even by February 1997, MCN was speculating confidently about a four-cylinder T600 to take on the middleweight super-sports market.

Bruno wouldn't be drawn further on future developments, so instead I asked him what Triumph would *not* be doing. One direction they certainly won't be venturing in is down-market: Triumph's customers are mostly mature, dedicated big-bike people, so the 125cc segment, for example, is best left to the Japanese: 'We couldn't make bikes at those sort of prices; we're not making any, BMW and Harley aren't making any, and although they may not look it, they are in fact a very specialist product – the Japanese concentrate on a big sector where there's a correlation of pounds to cc.'

In Japan they welcome a short run of 20,000 units or so because it keeps the

Model: T509 Speed Triple

Style   Cafe Racer

Engine
Type   Liquid-cooled, DOHC, in-line three-cylinder
Capacity   885cc
Bore/stroke   76mm × 65mm
Compression ratio   11.0:1
Induction   Electronic fuel injection, 41mm throttle body. Controlled by Sagem MC2000 computerized engine management system

Transmission
Primary drive   Gear
Clutch   Wet multi-plate
Gearbox   Six-speed

Electrics
Ignition   Digital, inductive type
Headlight   Two × 12 volt 60/55w halogen H4

Cycle Parts

Frame		Aluminium alloy perimeter, oval section aluminium extrusions; engine is additional structural member
Swinging arm		Aluminium alloy, single-sided with eccentric chain adjuster
Wheels	front	Brembo alloy three-spoke, 17in × 3.5in
	rear	Brembo alloy three-spoke, 17in × 6.0in
Tyres	front	120/70 ZR 17 Bridgestone Battlax BT56
	rear	190/50 ZR 17 Bridgestone Battlax BT56
Suspension	front	45mm forks with dual-rate springs, adjustable for compression, rebound damping and spring pre-load
	rear	Monoshock, adjustable for compression, rebound damping and pre-load
Brakes	front	Two × 320mm floating discs, two × four-piston calipers
	rear	Single 220mm disc, single two-piston caliper

Dimensions
Length   83in (2,115mm)
Width   28in (720mm)
Height   48in (1,230mm)
Seat height   31in (800mm)
Wheelbase   56in (1,437mm)
Weight (dry)   432lb (196kg)

Performance
Measured to DIN 70020
Maximum power   108bhp @ 9,100rpm
Maximum torque   85Nm @ 7,500rpm
Maximum revs   9,700rpm

Colours
1997 range   Lucifer Orange, Jet Black

Accessories   Integrated alarm system, carbon-fibre rear hugger, carbon-fibre front mudguard, carbon-fibre-look front tank panel, tank bag, paddock stand, flyscreen, handlebar conversion kit, seat cowl

Because it has no fairing and very little in the way of bodywork, the 1997 T509 Speed Triple is the lightest bike in the range, weighing in at a mere 432lb (196kg).

production line going in between the really big runs. Triumph couldn't make little bikes for the retail price of the Japanese, let alone for trade and export. The exceptions to the rule are the Italians, where small capacity bikes fit neatly under tax breaks. But these really are specialist machines, which is reflected in their price. The Japanese commuter bikes are at least £1,000 cheaper than Aprilia's race-rep RS125R costing £4,100; although to be fair, the Japanese race-reps such as the Honda NSR125R-R sell for similar money to the Aprilia. These kinds of bike have a limited market of course, complicated by high insurance prices for young riders, with Aprilia selling just two or three hundred units a year in the UK.

Higher up the size scale, Triumph is actually playing safe by going into the sports market. It is expanding rapidly, as is proven by the advance orders for the T595 Daytona: over 700 deposits were taken by UK dealers before its launch at the 1996 British Motorcycle exhibition. Over 180,000 visitors attended the NEC show, and as well as seeing the new models for the first time, were given their first taste of Triumph's 1997 range.

Triumph riders are mostly hardened enthusiasts, and there is no possibility that the company will attempt to increase sales by producing de-tuned machines to attract custom from the learner market in the light of the new riding-test format. Joked Bruno:

Triumph's sales and marketing operation was set up by Bruno Tagliaferri, left, talking in the dispatch bay with the author, who is attempting to negotiate a discount on a new Sprint.

If you were a learner, would you buy a castrated 750, or a 400? Triumphs are heavy bikes, and relatively expensive, and are just not appropriate for the inexperienced rider. We're selling to people who are well weathered and experienced. Young lads don't suddenly come and order an eight-grand Triumph, because they simply can't afford to. [Sadly, I reflected that some of the older ones can't, either.] It's an aspirational bike, and people who can't afford a new one are likely to buy a three-year-old Trident for around three-and-a-half to four grand. That way it's affordable and you can insure it third party. In any case, some people never buy new because of the initial depreciation, although Triumph's residual values are excellent.

This all adds up to a convincing argument, if not for selling your soul, then at least for arranging a loan from the bank.

4 Factory Tour

A Daytona T595 posed in the shrubbery outside the factory's smoke-glazed administration block. Naturally, visitors wouldn't normally find one there – but an Adventurer greets them in reception.

One of the great things about Triumph is its accessibility to enthusiasts. You can book up for one of the hugely entertaining guided tours given twice daily by Triumph front-man Robert Brown, who modestly describes himself as an out-of-work actor. The bikes are previewed over coffee with a showing of a factory video, and the tour ends with a questions-and-answers session. It is much to be recommended for a glimpse into how the bikes are made. Your local dealer may well organize a trip, or a visit can be arranged with Triumph.

The factory is divided into ten areas of operation, although there is some overlap: Stores, Goods inwards and Dispatch,

Machine shops, Welding shop, Paint shop, Chroming plant, Assembly shop, Test and Rectification. It is laid out in a series of long rectangular spaces: from right to left, the new Paint shop is at variance with the rest of the plant in being set well back and based on a north–south axis, while virtually everything else is east–west. Next along, and visually the most prominent, is the Administration section and canteen which fronts the far larger assembly shop. To the rear of this is the old paint shop and welding shop. To the left are the Dispatch and Stores areas, both of which have loading and unloading bays. Next to them are the three vast Machine shops – number three, containing the crankcase and cylinder head machining CNC equipment, runs the entire depth of the building. To the rear of Machine shops one and two is the Chroming plant. Fire exits and roller doors are strategically positioned all round the factory.

The reception area is sparsely furnished and businesslike in a modern, minimalist way: mirrors, chrome and black woodwork. A single Adventurer and Triumph-clad dummy form the decorative focal point, and visitors are welcomed by a single telephonist/receptionist. The conference room is to the right, where factory tours begin. On entering the plant from the reception area, the visitor is confronted by a couple of dozen sparkling new bikes, hot off the production line. Beyond them is the Assembly area, a confusing array of overhead gantries, conveyor belts, busy people in grey outfits, and half-recognizable bike components in the throes of construction. Amongst the clamour of metal-on-metal and whining air tools is the dimly heard background of Radio One, universal in all such working environments. However, everything, including conversation, is drowned out by the strident PA tannoy, which breaks in with tiresome regularity – with no offence to the receptionist – usually summoning individuals to the phone. The factory hooter announces break times, when the workers retire to their rest areas or to the canteen. But more of the Assembly shop later, because the production of the motorcycles actually starts off to the left of the line, with the stores, where components are sourced.

Smart and uncluttered, the reception area reflects the general efficiency of the factory; Jackie, the receptionist, also pages members of staff in the factory.

STORES

Because Triumph is constantly expanding, the current site is already at maximum capacity. Thus all spare parts and accessories not immediately required for production are stored and distributed from Triumph Spares, a satellite company operating from a separate building on the far side of the industrial estate. The Triumph production line operates on the now-typical 'just-in-time' or Japanese 'kan-ban' principle, so an appropriate quantity of componentry has to be held on site. This stock of parts is carried in the factory on lofty shelving, and can only be accessed by a very special fork-lift truck which elevates its operator some 40ft (12m) up to the upper shelves. The stocks are augmented by around sixty deliveries a day, involving something like two million items a month. Even so new Japanese parts orders can take three months to obtain, so careful ordering is crucial. Accordingly, Triumph holds fairly large stocks of suspension and carburettors.

As Japanese domestic component costs spiral, so Triumph is continually adjusting its calculations. Thus, the content of Japanese parts in Triumph machines is steadily reducing as the company makes more items for itself and locates suppliers closer to home; in fact it is now down to about 19 per cent. Japanese items also include switchgear and certain instruments, generators, gearboxes and clutches. A computerized bar-coding system is used to identify and source parts from the stores, and this is applied on the assembly line, too. There are over 9,000 locating points in the racking system, which has already been outgrown. When the new factory comes on stream, it is possible that the existing plant will simply become the spares and distribution centre.

QUALITY CONTROL

Beside the stores area is a white-painted office block where the inspection team is based: here, each component for every bike is checked prior to assembly on the

Shrouded bikes wait their turn for dispatch: the high-rise bars and chrome exhaust reveal this is an Adventurer.

co-ordinates measuring machine. They take the first product of each manufacturing process at the start of each shift. The equipment incorporates a sensitive computer-linked probe which scans and identifies the component – swinging arm, cylinder head, crankshaft or whatever – traverses its surfaces, measures relative distances, critical dimensions and recesses to the nearest micron, and detects any maladies or imperfections. There are 24.6 microns to 1,000th of an inch, and most aspects of Triumph manufacture are down to within five or six microns, which is far in advance of industry norms.

Elsewhere in the factory is the co-ordinates measuring machine's big brother. This is also housed in a separate booth, and is big enough to analyse a complete motorcycle if necessary, although it can also deal with minor components. There are four operators, two to each shift. To check something, the datum points are set according to the blueprints, then the operator picks some features which the machine can recognize every time it checks a particular component. The measurements are logged into the machine's computer. Then a programme is selected, and the probe independently traverses the part, which may be a crankcase for example, a frame sub-assembly or even a complete bike. Being larger, it is not quite as accurate as the smaller measuring device, although it can if necessary be used as a back-up to the smaller one.

Quality control is not limited just to co-ordinates measuring machines: there is also a so-called 'neighbour checking' system in operation, where individual workers are responsible for ensuring their mate has done his work properly. Although this may sound rather snide, in practice everyone takes the pragmatic view because it ensures that no mistakes are made. And according to dealers, since Triumph's warranty claims are a quarter of those received by BMW, who are renowned for their quality control, it demonstrates that not only the inspectors but the entire Hinckley workforce are doing an extremely good job.

PERSONNEL

The visitor is immediately aware of the relative youthfulness of the workforce; there are very few old-timers on the payroll, and the average age is around thirty. Everyone on the shop floor wears a low-key grey uniform, the type with stay-pressed trousers, except in certain environments where overalls are necessary. There are very few women at Triumph, partly because of the nature of the work – some of the jobs require considerable physical strength, besides which the company simply does not receive applications from women. In the Assembly shop there are just four women out of seventy personnel.

The factory is divided into departments, the departments into sections, and the sections into teams. The departments are defined by Administration, Machining, Assembly, and Research and Development, and within the Machining area are Goods inwards and Stores, Machine shop, Weld shop, Paint shop and Dispatch. Each section is in the charge of a supervisor who is responsible for, on average, six teams, and he answers to the production manager. Each team has a team leader, who is in effect a floating worker, an experienced and authoritative employee who is always on hand to assist with training, to take care of any problems, or to deputize should anyone be temporarily indisposed.

There are between six and eight workers – or 'operators', as they prefer to be called – in a team; any more than that and contact begins to suffer. The workforce is mobile,

Like pilgrims returning to the shrine, factory visitors are given twice-daily guided tours by Robert Brown, Triumph front-man; everyone is issued with earphones so his commentary can be heard, and to blank out the hubbub of factory activity.

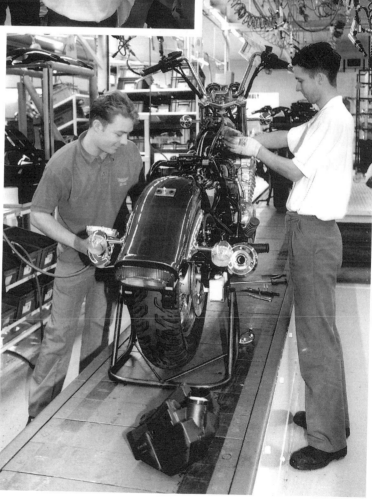

The workforce at Hinckley is, in the majority, relatively young – as can be seen from the 'operators' working on this Adventurer on Chassis 5.

too; people move from job to job in the factory and within teams so they build up an intimate knowledge of the production process and develop the skills necessary. One of the main benefits of this inter-plant mobility is that each worker has the opportunity of being personally involved in the construction of the complete bike, from Machine shop to Rectification. On the wall in each of the 'pig-pen' rest areas are skill matrixes, which illustrate the cross-section of talents and specializations within each team. Perhaps surprisingly, not many recruits come from elsewhere in the motor industry.

In the old days at Meriden, when output was running at 15,000 bikes a year, they employed about 1,250 people on the shop floor. Such is the efficiency of automation that in 1996 the whole staff at Hinckley amounted to 450 people.

Apart from crankshaft production and the Assembly line where only a single shift is worked, everywhere else in the factory operates on a two shift principle, from 6.00am until 2.15pm, and from 2.15pm until 11.15pm. On cranks and the Assembly line, working hours are from 8.00am to 5.00pm, with just half-an-hour for lunch, and one ten-minute break morning and afternoon. The management was apparently very good at utilizing the workforces' time to the full – yet I never saw even a suspicion of disgruntlement from amongst the workforce; quite the contrary in fact, and their enthusiasm was only too evident in a conversation I had with the Chassis 1 team leader, Rob Miller.

I used to work on the line at Jaguar and at Reliant cars, but Triumph is entirely different, and I've never once, in the four years I've worked here, got up in the morning and thought 'I don't really want to go'; instead, it's 'Great, let's jump in the car and go to work!' And that's not just me, that's genuinely the attitude of 99 per cent of the people who work here. We even like to meet up after work, because you can get a lot of discussion done over a pint in the pub.

Team leaders Guy Compton and Andy Bishop confer over the assembly of the T509 show bike.

A veteran of the old Meriden days, Albert Hamlett selects a length of exhaust tubing from stores.

This is true; Simon Clay and I encountered several groups of Triumph employees having an evening noggin in the nearby *Nag's Head* pub, and the subject never strayed very far from biking. Camaraderie is fostered within the factory, too: each team has its own 'pig-pen' within its own department, with a hot drinks vending machine, and there is an excellent works' canteen providing drinks, hot and cold meals and snacks, and where people can meet up and eat their sandwiches.

DAILY SCHEDULE

The daily schedule begins with a ten-minute meeting, during which team leaders inform their staff of any updates in the programme which have been called for by the production manager. Then there is a half-hour meeting with the supervisor to discuss anything applicable from the previous evening's shift. The production manager convenes regular meetings with supervisors to deliberate relevant issues, and the results are passed on to team leaders. Communication is all-important, in both directions, as the people on the line report back any observations they may have made during production.

The team leaders have feet in both camps, as it were: not only are they active on the production line, they are the vital link with the production manager. They also have opportunities to visit other UK-based motor manufacturers' production departments such as Toyota, Honda or Nissan, and may thus derive inspiration and improvements for Triumph.

To become a team leader could take two or three years, though it also depends on an individual's ambition as well as his aptitude; thus some people are brilliant fitters or mechanics, but simply wouldn't want the responsibility of leadership. For a team leader, one day may be taken up with line inspections, another with repair work. On

Mondays the team leaders have a separate meeting among themselves to iron out any problems and discuss topical issues.

Personnel at Hinckley are encouraged to come up with proposals for improving the factory environment and the production line in terms of safety and efficiency – as innovations such as the carburettor test facility testify. It is a very slick operation now, compared with the old days, and the workforce has helped to make it so. There is hardly anybody left from the Meriden days, and in fact there were only four 'old hands' back in 1983; the majority had either moved on, or retired.

Triumph is a firm advocate of training, and employees are always going off to follow various courses, usually engineering-linked. Naturally, all sections have their own specializations, and the workforce is as flexible and interactive as possible. In the Test and Rectification area, the bikes are nearing the point of no return, so the skills required are just that little bit more specialized; but instead of recruiting from outside the factory, the company draws people from elsewhere on the line with appropriate skills, and the gap left in that particular team will then be filled perhaps by someone recruited from outside the company, who will be trained up accordingly, working with fellow employees and the relevant team leader. Ideally, everyone can do his neighbour's job, and can therefore deputize or overlap where necessary. This concept is based on Japanese principles, and seems to work very well.

The annual factory holiday shut-down coincides with a thorough re-evaluation of the entire plant and a comprehensive refit and overhaul of machinery, as well as a repaint of wall surfaces. In August 1996 a week's shut-down provided for the reorganization necessary to bring on the new T595 and T509 models.

The supervisor's role is to ensure that everything happens as it should: inevitably it is less of a hands-on job. The supervisor of the Assembly shop is Steve Whatnall who used to be the line supervisor at nearby earth-moving giants, Caterpillar. He had this to say regarding the set-up at Triumph:

Supervisors have to do anything and everything. There are seven teams in Assembly, each with a team leader, and on average seven people in each team. The responsibility cascades down, really – each team looks after its own area, and basically it works very well because there is constant feedback both ways. The key thing about the company is communication, namely there is a series of meetings – the whole manufacturing department goes through a whole ritual of meetings. All the supervisors meet up at 4.45pm every day, together with the production manager, Paul Graves, for a feedback session. We discuss what's been built and the problems we've had, and what is coming up; and we will be given any information regarding future development.

Supervisors arrive at the factory at around 7.00am, to be ready for the early morning shift meeting – we get an awful lot of information back from these meetings. At 7.30am, half an hour before the start of the shift, we each have a meeting with our team leaders, and we explain to them what we've been told and what's especially relevant to them. Then at 8.00 o'clock, prior to the start of the track running, each team leader has a meeting with his group of people. Unless there have been specific problems to sort out, it is really to let them know what's going on in the rest of the company. It might be to let them know that the weld shop is having trouble with a particular robot. The benefit is that the more information you've got out, as soon as something goes wrong, the people building the bikes understand why. For instance, if the frame builder notices his stock of frames is a lot lower than it normally is, he will understand why if he's been told at the morning meeting that there's been a problem in the welding shop. He understands the reason, and he can react accordingly.

This was especially true when the workforce was waiting for the new models to commence production in November 1996. The building of 1996-spec models had finished, and the new Daytona and Speed Triple were to precede the rest of the 1997-spec range. People weren't exactly hanging around, because there were still stock and export orders to be fulfilled, but the situation wasn't normal, either. And although there may be less intimacy among the workforce than existed in 1991 when there were only 120 people there, nevertheless communication throughout the plant is as good as ever. Said Steve:

If there's a problem with welding, you can go and discuss it with the welding shop, or with the machine shop, or even sales for

that matter. There's always someone to talk to, so you can take everyone's point of view into account.

Other information to pass on might be to do with specification changes, or any special requirements on particular bikes; or staff changes, as people start or people leave. If absolutely necessary, supervisors are expected to help with the actual manufacture of the bike and its components. Steve observed:

There are seventy people in the assembly department, and I don't do as much as I'd actually like to do on the track. But that's not what I'm here for: to find out what they're doing is the most important thing. It's the team leaders who play a much more hands-on role. They are responsible for the layout of their area, with assistance from production engineers. Team leaders are the experts in their particular area of operation, and as well as being responsible for work allocation, they are expected to cover for holidays, sickness, or other departments, as well as run their section. The

The build docket containing the details of a bike's specification accompanies it right the way through the assembly process – as on this 1996 Daytona.

other thing is that you can't just step up to the line and pitch in. The lads are working a seven-minute cycle at the moment, and you don't learn a seven minute cycle that quickly. But if we had to, maybe two of us could do it, in an emergency.

So how does a new recruit get up to speed on the track?

First of all we'll bring the new person in, get him familiar with the area, and put him with someone who's experienced. We'll leave him with that person, and let him take on a little bit of the job at a time until he is comfortable. Then the 'old hand' just steps back and lets the new person get on with it. That could take anywhere from a week to a fortnight, maybe even longer. Meanwhile the team leader retains overall responsibility for making sure he is doing the job properly.

I remarked on the relative youthfulness of the workforce, and asked him whether it was a deliberate policy.

Recruiting and training people is very important; everyone being relatively young here is down to the nature of the company, because it's not been going that long. It wasn't a conscious decision not to employ older people, although we still have a few people from the old Meriden days. Basically, we advertise, and the sort of people you see here on the line are the ones who have applied. To some extent you're bound to attract the same sort of people, because part of the procedure is that the teams will actually have a big hand in who comes to work with them.

The way it works is that anyone who applies for a job at Triumph comes to spend a day at the factory. The applicant spends this day

working with a team, who judge his or her potential, and the supervisor finds out later if the team is happy for that person to join. This can be a daunting prospect, but actually it is quite realistic, since all concerned are going to have to get on with one another. The team itself does not have the final say, but if for some reason they took a dislike to the applicant, he or she would be very unlikely to get the job. If, however, the supervisor thought the applicant was acceptable, he or she would probably be directed somewhere else within the company. Thus it works both ways: by doing a day's work at Triumph, an applicant can

Entering the factory proper from reception, the visitor is greeted by ranks of sparkling, newly finished machines.

The co-ordinates measuring apparatus, being monitored here by Martin Harrison, is sufficiently versatile to log the dimensions of any component, such as a small section of engine casing or even a complete motorcycle if necessary.

(Below)
The factory operates on the now virtually standard kan-ban principle, where just the right number of components – such as these eccentric chain adjusters – are to hand 'just in time' for inclusion in the production process.

evaluate his or her prospects there, and this is an important factor because motorcycle manufacture is very different from most people's experience.

Once the new recruit has settled in, the company enquires how it might help improve his position. For example, he might be struggling at a work station because he happens to be left-handed and tooling has been set up for the previous operator who was right-handed – so an air tool can be relocated in a holster to make life easier. Or there may be a height difference, and the level of the bench may be uncomfortable – in which case the supervisor will get the bench height altered to suit, and racking can also be adjusted accordingly. So while operators cannot alter the production process, their immediate working environment can be adjusted.

While Triumph does not dwell on the company's past, there are one or two mementoes on display, such as this original Hinckley production engine, cast – rather than stamped – number 000001; it is a sixteen-valve 1,200cc Trophy unit, made on 6 February 1991.

(Below)
Most operations in the vast machine shop are robotized and computer-controlled, although the components are installed in the jigs by hand. Here is the downpipe welding cell in action.

Inevitably there is a certain amount of staff turnover, as in any factory where some functions are repeated incessantly; the rate of pay is a good incentive for operators to do repetitive jobs, but the boredom factor may be crucial in some cases. Even so, Steve Whatnall qualified this by saying: 'It may be hard work, repetitive and even tedious at times, but at the end of the day you've pro-duced a fantastic product, and one you can be proud of when you see it out in the street.'

Triumph's management are a modest bunch. Nobody was prepared to have his photo taken for the book. Commenting on this apparent reticence of senior Triumph people to become involved with any form of publicity, Steve said: 'We're happy doing what we're doing. The whole place works as

At the start of engine assembly, the Engine 1 team leader, Mark Thomas at right, checks the precise specification of each motor on the computer screen monitor.

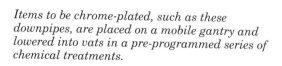

Items to be chrome-plated, such as these downpipes, are placed on a mobile gantry and lowered into vats in a pre-programmed series of chemical treatments.

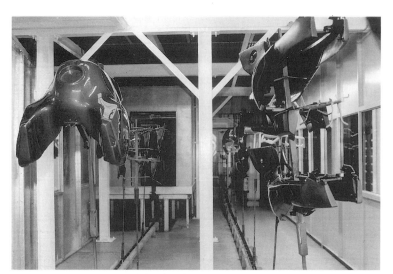

The newest facility at Hinckley is the paint shop, which has two separate tracks. Here, one set of bare panels goes in at the start of the process, while another freshly painted set – a Tiger tank – emerges from the drying oven.

On the assembly line, engines and wiring looms have just been installed in the chassis frames of an Adventurer and a Thunderbird.

Adventurers dangle from the overhead track during a break in proceedings; wheels and other ancillaries have just been fitted.

a team, and there are no ego problems; nobody's bothered about promoting themselves.' True enough, but characters abound among the workforce, and a number of them can be seen modelling for Triumph's superb brochures. But again: 'Although we're totally involved with building bikes here, we have to appreciate we're just part of the company. And we have to help the sales people, too, so if dealers and potential customers want to come round on the guided tours, the lads have instructions to accommodate them and to be polite, even if they *do* get in the way!' My experience while doing the photo shoots with Simon Clay was that everyone was unfailingly polite.

But do they put their money where their mouth is, so to speak? Several of the Triumph workforce are riders, and there is a generous staff discount on factory models. 'If you ride it for a year and then sell it, you'll get back what you paid for it,' said Steve, a Speed Triple rider. 'So you won't lose anything on the depreciation, and you might even make a bit of a profit! Between ten and fifteen bikes are sold "in house" each year.' This is quite a high proportion, considering the relative youth of the workforce and the difficulties of getting insurance on a 900 at a reasonable price. A 22-year-old will probably be looking at £1,000 to insure a Sprint, yet one or two have done it. But whether they ride them or not, everyone takes great pride in the product and seeing the shiny new bikes in dispatch gives the workforce a great feeling, because everyone has had some degree of input.

Those who do buy 'in house' can also specify their own bike, fitting non-standard parts or non-standard paint finishes:

provided the equipment has been tried and tested on something else within the range, and is compatible with the model being ordered, the employee can interchange componentry such as wheels or handlebars. It has to be approved by R & D, warranty and purchasing, but such customizing is acceptable. Frankly, I can't see why anyone would want to bother, since there is a Triumph model covering almost every aspect of travel the serious rider could wish for. But then, customizing a bike to one's own tastes has always held a certain fascination, and if you are on the spot to fix it up, well, why not? The staff also get the opportunity to run-in the press bikes before they go out, providing they have a full licence. This is usually on a one-day-over-the-weekend basis, and requires responsible riding, of course. And when it gets its hands on the bikes, the press has in the main been kind to Triumph, greeting new models with qualified optimism. When the new Daytona and Speed Triple were launched in October 1996, it was an excuse for unbridled praise and eulogy (*see* Chapter 7).

Both during and after assembly, bikes are subject to rigorous checks: here a Trophy is getting the 'once-over' from Rob Kean.

5 The Manufacturing Process

It is fascinating to study the methodology of Triumph's production line, to discover the logistics of what happens at what time in the process, and how it all dovetails together. A tour round the factory shows where many of the major parts begin life, and how they evolve into the bike's main components of frame, engine and suspension. To the workforce it is all relatively straightforward; to the uninitiated, watching these highly desirable products take shape is both entertaining and alluring. So compact and macroscopic is the factory, that the visitor can relate to it very easily. You can reach out and touch it, literally, as the tour guide hands over perhaps a manifold, a crankshaft, or a swinging arm for examination.

CHASSIS FRAME

The process is essentially the same for all models, although there are differences in construction and finish. An RT Adventurer, for example, is effectively a three-section frame; the front section comprises the main

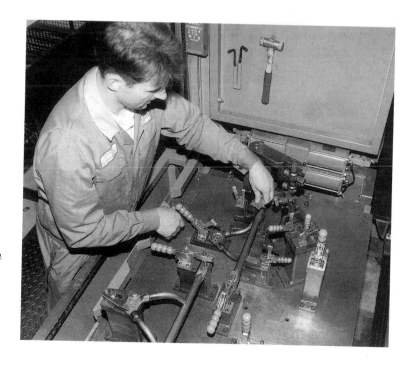

The seat-frame tubes are readied by Darren Stewardson in one of the subframe jigs for welding. Round tubing indicates this is for a Thunderbird or Adventurer; the rest of the range has square-section tube.

The robot welder is programmed to fuse the tubing together in Y-shaped sections, and the assembly builds up in stages. After each operation the table flips over to present another section – which could be for a different model.

The quality control area routinely checks one in five seat-frame sub-assemblies, starting with the first one every day.

spine and head-stock, the second is the seat frame, and the third section supports the rear mudguard. Bolts go through two holes to secure the rear mudguard's subframe, which is located in two other places. This is because of the cosmetic nature of the machine – being a single-seater, it is designed so that the subframe cannot be seen over the top of the mudguard; it is underneath it. With the Thunderbird on the other hand, being a two-seater, the seat subframe needs to go over the top of the mudguard, and it is effectively a two-section frame. These sections are united on the Assembly line by Chassis 1.

The standard black frame is the basis for the Trident 750 and 900, and until the 1996 model year change, it carried the original Daytona and Speed Triple. The same frame is finished in grey for the Sprint, simply for

With the frame mounted in a jig, the head-stock alignment is checked by Ian Goddard.

Team leader Richard Warren places tubing in one of the jigs in the cell which makes up exhaust manifolds.

cosmetics: its engine is grey, yet because it only has a cockpit fairing, the frame is visible, and therefore needs to match the engine. The Trophy has a frame all of its own, finished in grey, and not used on any other current models; and clearly the Tiger has a special frame, too. The new T595 Daytona and T509 Speed Triple have oval-section alloy twin-spar frames like the majority of Japanese sports bikes, incorporating two extruded aluminium tubes on either side of the engine.

Sparks fly in spectacular manner as the robot welder unites manifolding for the four-into-two junctions of the downpipes. The welding cells are fully encased, so their functions are not normally visible to anyone except the operator.

For obvious reasons the frame has to be very strong, having to cope with between 98 and 147bhp (at the gearbox) – yet the frame weighs just 26lb (12.5kg). The main tube of the spine frame is made of micro-alloy steel, and actually comes from Japan for cost reasons, although an economic European source is possible. It arrives in pre-cut lengths, and it is formed, cut, and welded into shape by robots in the factory's small welding shop. Frame castings for the T595 and T509 alloy chassis are made by PBM in Birmingham, and welded up and finished at Triumph.

The rear swinging arms are made on three CNC machines in the auxiliary machine shop, which is staffed by only three fitters. The swinging arm begins life as pre-cut lengths of extruded aluminium section, also made by PBM, becoming a box-section item which eventually houses the eccentric rear chain-adjuster. The Thunderbird and Adventurer models have oval-section swinging arms. The Enshu and Matsura machine tools are highly sophisticated devices; the Enshu has a sliding tool base which can fabricate two pairs of swinging arms at once, and can accommodate either flat- or oval-section side rails. The Matsura also has two alternating tool areas, and is capable of machining two pairs of box-section swinging arms at the same time. Other items such as clutch covers are also made here. In the newest, largest and most versatile Cincinatti machine, three sections are handled at one time. One person checks the quality control before the machined items proceed to the robot welder. They include the cross-braces for the various models, and the subtle differences are more clearly apparent at this point than when they are installed in the bike. All are derived from the same swinging arm, but the Tiger's differs from the Trident and Daytona derivatives, while the Thunderbird's beefier oval section is different again.

The machine shop team leader Matt Jones and Adrian Turvey, right, programming one of the bar-feed CNC lathes. Live tooling like this can perform more than one function.

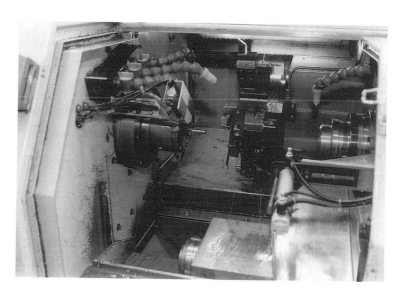

The business end of a twin-spindle CNC lathe; there are sixteen lathes altogether in the machine shop, milling about 110 different components – this is enough for a whole week's production.

Batches of machined components await their turn to be taken off to the next stage in the assembly process; before this they will all have been deposited in a vat for de-greasing, followed by a cold wash, and lastly a hot wash. There is a large number of robot welders in the factory, quite as many as you would find in any high-tech operation, and many of them are brand new, although their life expectancy is only about five years, such is the pace of technology. The new factory up the road will be full of brand new CNC machines, and although twice the size of the current plant, it is likely to be staffed by the current workforce. As it is, the current level of automation has expanded dramatically in the last four years.

Swinging arm production continues like this: an alloy MIG machine contains the robot welder at its centre, and will fabricate items such as side rails, forward pivot and rear wheel adjuster. Once the tool table is loaded up, the operator initiates the process and the robot arm swings across and welds up the exposed top sections. The tool table then flips through 180 degrees so the robot can weld up the sections previously underneath. On the desk in the centre of the robot station is a small red jig with probes which carry out an alignment check. As long as the probes touch at relevant points, the shape must be good. After checking, the components are date-stamped, and given a shift number for reference in the event of any future problem. The side rails are then placed in another welding station to be mated with the cross-brace, flipping over as before to get both sides done.

The operator then takes the finished swinging arm to a cleaning station where any imperfections in the weld are cleaned off with a hand tool – and therein lies a certain incongruity, the fact that the high-tech robot's work has to be finished off by hand with files, hammers and checking gauges.

The components are then hung up on racks, literally to rest, so the stresses imposed on the metal during the welding process can dissipate.

After checking, the swinging arms go off on a pallet to GEC in Leicester to be highly polished and anodized black; after re-inspection, they then return to the production process.

ENGINE MANUFACTURE

The modular system was very important to Triumph's renaissance, enabling them to get up to speed as quickly as possible, producing a wide model range of fifty bikes a day within two years. That was the break-even point, when it was clear that the company was viable.

Triumph uses the same conrods as virtually all other top motorcycle manufacturers, with the exception of BMW. A combination of machines hones the conrods to shape, including a stone tumbler which deburrs them. Scratches are removed, but cracks naturally result in immediate failures. Another machine buffs all the facets of the finished conrods on a pair of polishing wheels, which helps to ensure that they are perfectly balanced.

The cranks and cams are drop-forged units manufactured in Germany, and there is much work to be done when they are profiled at Hinckley – after all, if an engine is to run smoothly, there is no substitute for a precisely machined crank. The cam lobes are pre-hardened at the foundry, but are ground by Triumph. A single raw camshaft provides the model for three different Triumph cams as the lobes are ground to different heights and shapes. They are designated red, blue and green, with the red cam the most extreme high-lift unit for the Super III.

MACHINE SHOP

One of the most recent departments to be set up within the factory, and the most rapidly expanding, is the vast machining section. The machines here cost a staggering £7m, and it took Japanese suppliers Enshu eighteen months to build them. There are two lines of machines, nearly 328ft (100m) long, operated by just six people under supervisor Dick Harrison, with four running the crankcase line on the left and two on the cylinder head line to the right.

All Triumph's engine castings – blocks, heads and covers are made by Zeus Engineering in West Bromwich – go straight to the Paint shop where they are inspected, then impregnated with a resin-based pigment. This improves the porosity resistance of the castings, and is virtually standard practice throughout the industry. While the Thunderbird and Adventurer engine cases are left naked, the rest are powder-coated black or grey for durability and finish: those of the Daytonas, Tridents and Tigers are black, while the Sprints and Trophys are grey. Modular construction means that one size fits all triples, and another cylinder means it's a four.

Back in the Machine shop, an engine starts life when an operator takes a pair of crankcases, top and bottom, faces off the two mating surfaces and bolts the two halves together. Then they are machined as a matched pair, and not split again until all the machining is finished. Internal markings guarantee that the halves never lose track of one another. It takes a mere forty-five minutes to prepare, machine and pressure-test, and finish a crankcase; this sounds quick, and indeed it is, because there are no fewer than twelve separate machining processes involved in transforming bare engine casings into assembly-ready components.

The right-hand row is the cylinder-head production line, and despite the amount of work involved in forming the ports and channels, it takes only two hours to

Crankcases come in two halves, and are machined as matched pairs.

complete a cylinder head ready for assembly. The heads spend about ten minutes in each machine, the first phase being where the rough edges of the castings are faced off. Once the bottom 'fire face' is pared smooth, the operator has a datum point for the rest of the head's dimensions and a multitude of tiny machining operations follows. The location pin holes are drilled first; then threads are tapped, and line boards inserted in the aluminium where the camshaft runs. The machines are capable of great accuracy; for example, the bucket cam followers are machined to within seven microns.

After machining, the castings are individually pressure-tested for porosity in a liquid bath to four bars for four minutes. Any fault in the casting is likely to have been exposed during the machining process. When the castings have passed the porosity check, they are united with valve seats and guides which have been waiting in liquid nitrogen, in which the metal actually shrinks due to the intense cold of minus 118°F. Once knocked into position, the metal warms up and takes a vice-like grip within the head.

The next machine simultaneously reams out the valve guides and cuts the three facets of the valve seats. The final stage prior to assembly is cleaning in the crankcase wash.

As Triumph volumes increased, some suppliers found it difficult to keep up with both quality and quantity, and Triumph had to become more self-sufficient; its chromium-plating plant came on stream just in time to finish the glitzy Thunderbird. Chromed items include the downpipes, made in house, the megaphone silencers, made by Burgess, and the ancillaries such as mirrors and indicator housings by Birmingham pressed steel specialists J. J. Engineering. Suppliers of other engine components, such as those for the T595, include Sage Aluminium (sump), Magnes Castings (engine covers), Polydynamics (oil pipes), Texplastics (oil strainer), Scandura (gaskets and seals) and Motad (silencers).

THE CHROMIUM PLATING PLANT

Each part of the factory has its own atmosphere, and not surprisingly, the chrome-plating plant is tinged with a chemical aroma. It is also noisy because of the highly efficient extractor fans. Installed in 1994 at a cost of £1.3m, this fully automated, state-of-the-art facility occupies a large section of the factory, considering that the items processed here are relatively small ones. It is almost 50yd long by 25yd wide (45m by 23m), with two raised parallel rows of rectangular galvanized tubs extending all the way down the room.

The items to be chromed are subjected to a stringent succession of dips, purges and electric shocks. For example, manifold downpipes, direct from the welding shop, are first cleaned up and clipped onto a jig; the plant operator sets the programme on the computer monitor, and the consignment is sent on its way. Different objects are set to different programmes according to surface area, although the computer system is sufficiently flexible that they can mix and match. Thus the jig may contain two sets of downpipes and one set of balance pipes, or any combination.

There are two different processes; one for mild steel, and the other for stainless steel. All the headers, whether they are to be bright chrome or black chrome, are stainless steel. To go from black chrome to bright chrome is an immediate process, but to go the other way round means clearing the whole system. Therefore they deal with the black chrome objects first thing in the morning, and move on to the bright work later, whether it be

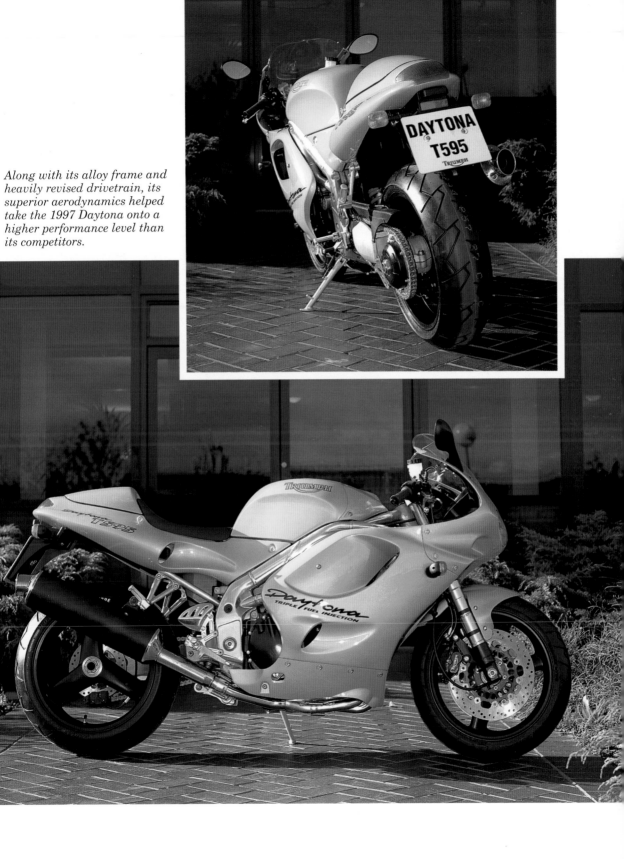

Along with its alloy frame and heavily revised drivetrain, its superior aerodynamics helped take the 1997 Daytona onto a higher performance level than its competitors.

Racing improves the breed, as well as providing glamour, sexy bikes and a host of thrills. This bike was Michael Rutter's during the 1996 Speed Triple Challenge season.

(Below) Crated and boxed up in dispatch: a 1996-spec Speed Triple and a Daytona shortly to leave the factory for delivery.

(Above) With the trend towards the stripped-down street-fighter look in the mid-nineties, Triumph's T509 Speed Triple was right on the button stylistically, whilst technologically its advanced specification lifted the Café Racer segment to fresh heights.

(Above) An Adventurer, a Thunderbird and a Tiger in the making have just had their engines mated with their chassis frames.

The entry-level Trident is the most unassuming model in the range, because its unfaired and unpretentious looks make no ambiguous claims about performance or touring potential. But it is capable of responding to either task if required, and can be defined as something of a wolf in sheep's clothing.

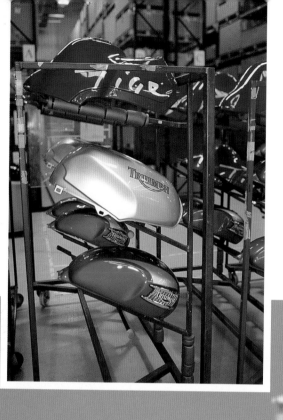

After polishing, freshly liveried tanks for Tiger, Trident and Thunderbird sit on racks outside the painting booths, awaiting transfer to the assembly line.

(Below) As a prospect for export, the Thunderbird found a great many riders all over the world who fell for its classic roadster looks.

(Above) *Out on the open road, the Adventurer is all about relaxed cruising, as well as extrovert posing when riding in town.*

(Inset) *The Adventurer's 855cc three-cylinder performance is rated at 70bhp, which is more than ample for its classic-inspired road manners. This 1996 bike is finished in Heritage gold and ivory, with hand-painted black coachline.*

The instrument binnacle and controls of the T509 Speed Triple are a model of austerity, ranging from clearly legible black-on-white dials and warning lights, to regular Triumph switchgear.

The Trophy's role as Triumph's staple touring bike was confirmed when the model was substantially revamped in September 1995 to include curvaceous fairings and matching panniers.

The Sprint was introduced in 1992, and its main attributes of agility and torque, together with its wind-cheating cockpit fairing, made it a peerless performer as a sports-tourer.

The Tiger is an excellent all-rounder. As befits its enduro styling, it performs well on rough tracks, and it also makes a fine long-distance touring machine. Its long-travel suspension soaks up road surface deformities, and its elevated riding position gives good visibility in traffic.

In amongst the Speed Triples in the paddock, with the Francis Williamson/Rafferty Newman and Michael Rutter/Market Motorcycles bikes in the foreground.

(Below) Alan Batson gets his knee down during a Donington round of the 1996 Mobil One Speed Triple Challenge. He finished the season in third place.

(Below) The Mobil One Speed Triple Challenge was supported by much of the dealer network. This is Francis Williamson's machine, run by Fareham, Hampshire UK dealers Rafferty Newman.

(Above) *Launched in Paris in September 1995, the cruiser-styled Adventurer showed just how confident Triumph was of success in this niche market. Note the high-rise bars and duck-tail rear mudguard.*

(Below) *From its gorgeous aluminium-alloy oval-tube frame and three-spoke Brembo wheels to its twin-pod headlights and flyscreen, the 1997 T509 Speed Triple is a lean, mean machine indeed.*

downpipes or air boxes or whatever. The rest of the work is mostly mild steel, and this determines which process tanks they go into; the mild steel items spend two-and-a-half hours in the chroming process. Everything defers to the kan-ban system, so items to be chromed are treated in strict order of production requirement.

Side one's process tanks range from acid-based cleaners and etchers to anodic purifiers. An overhead mechanical hoist lifts the jig into tank one, containing an alkali-based soap cleaner, the first of seven processes. There follow two rinses, designed to avoid cross-contamination between tanks. Then the jig is lowered into an aggressive sulphuric and phosphoric acid-based anodic cleaner, which is like plating in reverse; a charge is put through the components and this removes any contaminants. Then the jig enters a blow station to be dried, and immediately heads into the electro-polish, another anodic system which agitates the metal and makes the items bright and shiny. This is a good basis for applying the nickel coating. As they emerge dripping from this tank, the jig's contents are an extraordinary reptilian green colour. A

couple of rinses follow, then a hydrochloric acid plunge which etches the surface to provide a good 'key' for the nickel.

Then the jig enters the first of the nickel process tanks, known as the nickel strike, which amounts to a very thin base coat. The actual plating process occurs when a rectifier puts a charge through the objects on the jig, and nickel contained in baskets hanging on one side of the tank is attracted onto the components suspended in the centre.

The jig is then dipped into a rinse, hoisted across the top on its conveyor, and down side two where it will receive the rest of the nickel coats. There are three nickel baths: the first coat is semi-bright, followed immediately by bright nickel, then a micro-porous nickel. Next it is time for another two rinses, and then the decorative bright or black chrome coat is applied. Compared with the amount of nickel that has already gone on, this is a very thin layer, only about one micron deep. The nickel coats amount to roughly eighty microns, and will provide all the corrosion protection the components will need. The last part of the process is the chrome neutralizer, which has the effect of removing the residue left on the components, and it drains off in a

The chrome- and nickel-plating plant comprises some seventeen tanks, and items such as these downpipes are dunked into the chemicals and rinses by overhead gantry.

green liquid. Then a couple more rinses will ensure the components are clean, the last of these being a hot tub. Finally five minutes in a hot air-drying station completes the journey.

The black-chromed downpipes and balance pipes need a 'helping hand' when they come off the jigs, because the cleft between the pipe-joins somehow always misses out on the electrolysis, and has to be finished by hand by the operator using a spray gun.

Keeping the system clean is a rigorous maintenance programme, which includes changing the rinses on a daily basis to avoid cross-contamination. The changes occur at the end of the night shift – the plant operates from 6.00am to 11.15pm, and it starts to be closed down two hours before the end of the shift. An effluent-control system monitors the waste chemicals and impurities, and heavy metal contaminants are disposed of by specialists.

After leaving the chrome-plating plant, the items go to the polishing room, where a mirror finish is obtained on any area which will ultimately be visible on the finished bike. There is nothing more unsightly than corroding chrome, so Triumph's bright-work is subjected to 1,000 hours under a salt spray, which simulates ten years' road use.

The only chromed parts not plated in house are those sourced elsewhere, such as instrument bezels and indicator stalks, and mountings for the retro models – and predictably, these are the only chromed bits with which there have been problems.

CRANKS

The drop-forgings which form the cranks take shape in one area of the machine shop. The four-cylinder crank is the same item as the three-cylinder, but the forging undergoes severe contortions during its conversion from the four- to the three-cylinder version.

Crankshafts start life as drop-forgings, and although the same billet is used for the three- as the four-cylinder motor, it goes through a number of additional contortions to create the triple's crank.

Like wood, steel has a grain of sorts running through it. The cranks start life as long steel sausages and are die-stamped into crank-shape, with big ends set at 180 degrees; on a four-cylinder engine this spaces the power forces equally. Seams down either side indicate where the sides of the mould came together in the stamping. On the three-cylinder crank, the big ends are at 120 degrees so as to space the power forces equally. They are drop-forged as regular four-cylinder cranks, but while they are still at forging temperature, they are twisted twice through 60 degrees to obtain the right configuration. The mould seam can be traced along what is now a very tortured path, and the steel is now so unstable that after initial machining, the cranks are sent away to be stress-relieved.

There is more work to be done on a crank than perhaps one might imagine. On their return, the rest of the crank manufacture continues on a series of lathes. The three- and four-cylinder cranks are on separate machines; the Heller cuts all the ends and mains, and they are then de-burred. The run-out of the crank is taken down to five microns, the big-ends and mains are taken down to five or six microns, then the gear teeth are profiled, along with balancing and hardening.

The machine which cuts the gear teeth is the Churchill RK11. To begin with the cogs have sharp, saw-blade teeth, but these are smoothed off by a rolling helical gear. In fact at the time of writing the ageing Churchills were being replaced by the Pfauter, which is altogether more sophisticated, and can be programmed not only to cut the teeth but also to reprofile them.

Next comes the machine which balances the crankshafts. Originally cranks were sent away to be balanced, but Triumph discovered that they could do the job four times more accurately if they bought a particular

machine. The machined cranks are placed in the machine, and they are rotated at 7,500rpm – not especially fast, but sufficient to identify where balancing is required. The computer-gauging machine identifies where adjustments are needed, and a drill progresses over the mains along the crank, removing just the right amount of material from the balance webs where required. An allocated bar-code identifies the particular crank so that it will be recognized when it arrives on the production line, and will be fitted to the right crankcase.

At the end of the machine shop are the two cylindrical plasma-nitriding ovens (these cost the company £400,000 each), where Triumph cranks are treated. Amazingly, in the whole of the world's motor industry, only Triumph, Porsche and Mercedes-Benz possess nitriding ovens; everyone else sends theirs out to specialists. Once machined up and balanced, cranks are placed on a two-tier cradle in batches of forty-two at a time, in a thirty-hour case-hardening process. The canopy is lowered and sealed and a vacuum created within the oven, when a heady mix of hydrogen and nitrogen is pumped in and ignited at 1,176°F (540°C). Two pairs of probes establish that the process is happening at the right temperature. The soot deposit is cleaned off, and one crank is taken at random for crack testing on a Vickers analyser, before the rest are taken off for polishing.

Visually, this is possibly the most accessible machine, as you can actually stand there and see it happen: a swirl of yellow liquid and a swift round and back again, and the facets are polished. Most CNC machines are inaccessible without special co-operation from management and operator. Next, a co-ordinates measuring machine checks the crank with a probe the size of a needle, and any anomalies are immediately evident, within microns, to the operator who is studying the procedure on a computer screen.

Only two other motor manufacturers have a plasma-hardening facility. Forty-two cranks spend thirty hours here in a heady cocktail of hydrogen and nitrogen.

(Inset) Newly milled cranks are placed in one of two plasma-nitriding chambers by Gary George.

Once hardened, cranks are cleaned and polished with fluids in this multi-belt machine.

Each facet of the crank is checked for imperfections on this co-ordinates measuring machine, and any anomalies are picked up on the computer screen.

TURNING SHOP

Here, items such as the head-stocks and cylindrical balance shafts are machined up from pre-cut lengths of drop-forged steel billet. Triumph has gone against the trend by doing more and more of its own milling and turning, down to the smallest nuts, bolts and washers. This is partly because these items are relatively expensive to source elsewhere, and because the Midlands-based companies which used to make them have either disappeared or now make something else.

Lengths of steel tube are supplied by McReady's foundry in standard 3m (10ft) and 5m (16ft 5in) lengths which arrive on a fork-lift truck and are craned into store by hoist. Triumph have sixteen Japanese-made, bar-feed, live-tooling lathes with German hand controls. There are two kinds: one with automatic multi-load feed, and another which has to be loaded individually. They have one or two spindles and so can perform two functions, and a variety of tool heads, producing 110 different items in quotas sufficient for a week's production; stock rotation is kept to a minimum in the interests of flexibility, so that no stock runs out before a design change is implemented. Previously there was nearly always an excess of raw material, which tied up large amounts of capital unnecessarily – phosphor bronze is a particularly expensive commodity at £300 per 3m (10ft) bar, and it is only used for the thrust washers on the four-cylinder motor's balance shaft. McReady's are now supplying just three phosphor-bronze lengths a week.

The methodology is straightforward: every box for the raw material has the part number stamped on it. The box is taken to the machining station, the components are used, and the finished articles deposited in the kan-ban box. This is placed in a stillage, and is then transferred to stores where it is bar-coded; it is now ready for withdrawal into the production process. The box is returned to the turning area with raw materials in, making for a constantly controlled flow of production; this is a relatively new methodology for Triumph.

To execute the turning process, the operator places a 3m (10ft) length into the breech, and as it is drawn through the lathe the tool head machines the component – a bar-end weight, for example – then spins it, drops it off and feeds it out. The machine then ushers in another section of raw material, and the process continues while a pile of swarf gathers at the back end. There are two sizes of twin-spindle, live-tooling lathe: the larger ones simply accommodate bigger diameter raw materials and produce bigger diameter components. The CNC machines are about four-and-a-half-years old, and are likely to be replaced when production moves to the new plant. When volumes go up, the whole game will be raised again.

Apart from steel, there are some components in stainless steel and aluminium, such as the concentric adjusters for the rear swinging-arm, and in most cases the aluminium bits are sent out to be anodized against corrosion. Some high quality aluminium comes from the States, and the remainder from Germany. Most of the steel components are electro-plated for protection as well as appearance, and are subjected to a rigorous test of 240 hours under a continuous salt spray – which is twice as long as Japanese standards. By way of comparison, Triumph regularly buy in a range of US and Japanese components and subject them to similar tests, and usually Honda's come out best: 350 hours is about their limit before deterioration starts, as compared with Triumph's own parts which can be pushed to 550 hours before problems start to show.

The down side of electro-plating is that while it may look smart, the part is also rendered more brittle by the process. Thus, some of Triumph's electro-plated bolts are not given so great a coating.

WELDING SHOP

The welding shop is tucked away in a corner of the main machine area, and is staffed by just five people. Here, the chassis-frame components are fused together by computer-controlled MIG welders, including the main spine, the box sections and the subframes. The chassis tubes are formed from pre-cut lengths by a machine which achieves the right geometry. Every single piece has to fit perfectly into a pre-production-checking jig.

The main robot-welders which create the frame components are housed in big green containers, and are the biggest in the factory. Two robots work together in the main cell, walking up and down in unison along the centre line. Each half of the robot has four tool-tables, which flip over, making eight working faces in each end of the cell. As the robots move from the left- to the right-hand side of their section, they steadily assemble four different subframes, spot-welding at pre-determined strategic points as they go. Since Triumphs now have five different subframes, a new ABB welder has been installed. Two differing types of subframe – bolt-on and weld-on – are made on either side of the machine's tool-tables: thus you have a Thunderbird on one side; flip through 180 degrees, and you have an Adventurer, both of which are bolt-on frames. The sections grow almost organically with each successive weld process, while seat and tank bridges are added later. After checking on datum points, they are placed on a rack for fixing to the main frame. The Sprint, Trident and Trophy

have different tubes to the Tiger, but all use square tubing, whereas the Adventurer and Thunderbird use round tube. The bikes' seat rails and drop rails build up to become a pair of box-section Y-piece subframes, then they disappear into the far corner in cell two where they are welded onto the back of the main spine. It will also have front and rear engine mountings and swinging arm fixings attached.

It takes seven-and-a-half minutes of actual work time to create a single chassis-frame. The robot machines have a built-in fail-safe device which means they cannot work if the gas supply is not turned on, for instance, and if the doors are not locked shut. Every morning and afternoon, the supervisor takes a complete frame from each batch for checking on a master-sample jig for weld quality, alignment and locating holes, and once they are approved, they are packed off to an outside firm to be shot-blasted and de-greased. After dunking in rust killer and inhibitor, the frames are then totally immersed in paint; close inspection reveals vent holes which allow the paint access to the inside surfaces of the frame.

When the frames return to the factory, areas which will be visible on the finished bike are given further treatment, and the complete frame is then powder-coated.

The downpipes are manufactured here too, in four robot cells, growing in a complicated succession of welds into the finished system. A Swedish machine tool forms the bends for the three- and four-branch manifolds as required, in both small- and big-bore versions, and a separate jig checks that every system is accurate. With the exception of the lightweight three-into-one sports system, all exhaust downpipe systems are made in-house, from high-frequency, welded stainless-steel piping, pre-cut to length before delivery by Sabring in Germany.

THE PAINT SHOP

Triumph's paint process went in-house in 1996, and is based on a two-pack isocyanate system. It is a miniaturized version of a car plant's paint shop, minus the robots, and is similar to that used by Harley-Davidson; the American firm was actually instrumental in setting up the Hinckley plant's paint shop. Some new and complex scrubbing systems have been installed to catch stray air-borne particles, and to make the plant as environmentally clean as currently possible, bearing in mind the new water-based technology waiting in the wings. The area involved is surprisingly large, with a slow-moving track conveying the items to be painted through the different parts of the process. The fairings and panels are prepared before being hand-sprayed in sealed booths, stoved, checked and polished – which makes this one of the most labour-intensive areas of production. In its way, it is as much of a production line as the main Assembly area.

The spray booths are basically the same as are used in a car-body plant, on a smaller scale; from a single booth, Triumph now has five, each with a glass front the size of a small shop window. A moving track was necessary both for ease of spraying and to control the pace of the operation. Now at least twice its original size, the current paint shop came on stream on 19 August 1996. The track has also evolved and extended to keep up with the capacity of the spray booths and to feed the finishing booths.

Interestingly, Triumph uses the conventional spray-painting method for its fairing panels, rather than the self-colouring method employed by firms such as Caterham and Lotus where the paint goes into the fibreglass mould first before the matting and resin. The advantage with a painted panel is that small blemishes can always be repaired and painted over, whereas any damage to a self-coloured panel means the whole thing has to be resprayed because the original paint finish is locked into its surface.

Watching Paint Dry

At Triumph there is a half-serious internal fine system – a bit like a swear-box – for not wearing overalls in the Paint shop, and similarly if you are caught wearing a ring or a wrist-watch while working: the potential for jewellery to damage paintwork is very real. So not wishing to contribute our 20p each to the fine box, cameraman Clay and I donned the standard-issue overalls and were given a tour of the paint shop by supervisor John Bradley. We recognized him as another member of Triumph's unofficial Nag's Head social club which we had discovered on an earlier factory visit. He told us he had just sold a Speed Triple, because of the uncertainty of its value when the new T509 was in the dealers. John has eight team leaders working under him, four on each shift, and described the layout of his territory: 'There are two identical lines, with very subtle differences. One runs clockwise, while the other goes counter-clockwise. One is more awkward to follow, because two booths and an oven were located in the centre of what was previously the preparation area,' he explained. True, it made the line of posts bearing the fairings and panels rather hard to track as it zig-zagged through the various booths, although as they emerge from the booths, disappear into the dark ovens and thence on to the next stage, you have a clear image of progression. In a strange way it reminds the visitor of a museum, where you go from one display case to another, peering in at the exhibits, or perhaps a zoo is a better analogy, since some of the exhibits are animated. Whatever, along with the chroming plant, it is one of the most consistently noisy areas in the factory because of the various blowers and extractors.

'We divided the paint shop into line one and line two, and then prep and paint,' said supervisor Bradley; 'Those four areas are convenient from a work point of view, but perhaps not so convenient for people control; that's because the people in the paint booths are driven by the speed of the track.'

Before the panels are painted they are taken off trolleys and unwrapped from their transit packaging by prep station 1. Most panels and mudguards have been sourced from the fibreglass moulding specialist Acerbis in Milan, fuel tanks come from Italy and Germany, while Trident panels are made in Coventry, and some mudguards come from Stratford-on-Avon. Triumph started using Acerbis in the early days when volumes were relatively low, but as production has increased, the Italians have kept pace. The panels are prepped-up and pegged onto the posts which will carry them through the painting process. In general terms it takes five hours to paint all the panels for one bike, and this is divided into several different

stages. Clearly some require more work than others, depending on the level of detail or the expanse of fairings to be done. The Tiger, Adventurer and Thunderbird panels spend more time in preparation than they do in painting, which creates slight logistical problems, because there will be gaps in the paint booths. In terms of peg spaces, an enduro, as they call the Tiger in the factory, takes 16.25 minutes to paint; a Thunderbird takes 6.25 minutes, but the setting up of special effects and coachlining takes twice that long. By mid-day on our Paint shop tour, they had done eighty tanks for these machines, some for spares, some for the build, and some for Triumph America, and this was thought somewhat exceptional. The main reason was the anticipated commencement of the T595 and the T509 build. Normally they are dealing with a variety of bikes across the whole range, and they time it so that a mixture of parts goes down the line, sometimes in sets destined for a particular bike or to fulfil stock orders. But if a run

Panels are mostly sourced from Acerbis in Milan. They are prepared before painting, with sharp edges trimmed, and blemishes filled and rubbed down.

A Tiger *tank is about to receive a colour coat; painters are fully masked and hooked up to air lines, while a cascading backdrop of water catches overspray.*

(Below) *Fine attention to detail includes cleaning off any specks or runs using cotton swabs and solvent.*

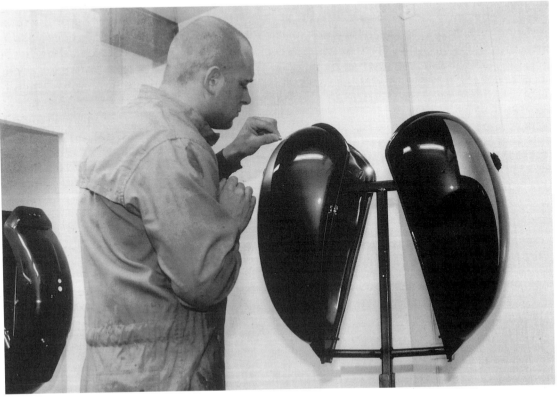

of say, tanks, goes down because of a lengthy order for a particular colour, the painters at the special effects stage of the process will be struggling to keep up.

At the start of the line are the ionized blowers, which fittingly are accompanied by a loud wind noise, and rid the panels of particles of static electricity. In the early days, this function was gallantly performed by a man with an impregnated rag, wiping down the bare panels. This was found to cause more problems than it cured, and he was superseded with the installation of £20k-worth of electrostatic equipment.

The first two booths are where the primer and base coats are applied. These are two-man operations, where one goes round the edges of the panel, while the other concentrates on the main surface area. The base coat will never go off; even after a week, the panel can be wiped clean. It has to be sealed with a coat of clear lacquer, which happens in the next booth along. Such is the speed of the track that the painter gets roughly three minutes to cover each panel – though you get the impression they are not hanging about, anyway. Until now, the panels have a very dull finish where the base coat is flashed off, but the lacquer starts to transform their appearance. An exception going through during our tour was a one-off yellow enduro panel set, destined for a German Automobile Association Tiger, and being in two-pack paint, it remained shiny in primer.

The next stage is the so-called flamboyant booth, which is only used if special finishes are to be applied, one colour on top of another. Triumph's most experienced painters work here, as well as in the clear coat booths – although most of the time it is just an empty chamber. In each of the paint booths, the painters work with a backdrop reminiscent of Niagara falls, as water cascades down the back wall of the booth into a pool of foaming white water. This wash screen collects all the surplus paint spray particles which didn't land on the panel, and smashes them over a matrix of weir plates, sluicing out the paint from the water; the pigment drains down into a chamber beneath the booth, and the water is recirculated. In the miniature labyrinth of the paint booths the floor is kept wet to keep any dust down.

The environment within the paint booths is further controlled by monitored air flow. An equilibrium is achieved by balancing the influx of air through ventilation and the actual spray guns, against an extractor at the rear. This creates a still environment which is vital to obtaining a perfect finish; too much extraction and heat would be lost from the oven, or all the paint from the base coat might be sucked through onto the clear coated parts. Too little extraction, and the process would be upset by too much turbulence and paint would be taken up the silhouettes.

Naturally the painters are fully masked and wear respirators in the booths. Their masks are fed by lines from outside the booths. More air is fed in than the painter actually breathes, and the surplus is blown out at the sides of the mask. This equipment is a legal requirement where isocyanate paints are used, as they can cause asthma. The painters' lungs and breathing capacity are checked for 'puff' every six months or so, to ensure their health remains good, although even having a cold may mean they will fail the test.

Using spray guns means a superb finish is obtained, actually far superior to the average car's paint job, where the pitted orange-peel effect is prevalent due to distances of surfaces from the robot spray heads. In some of the more specialized car plants – TVR, or Morgan for instance – everything is sprayed in primer and then the vehicle is flatted down, followed by the base coat and clear coat. The disadvantage of this is that it will inevitably introduce a lot of dust into the system. At Triumph

An enduro tank nears the end of its journey through the painting process.

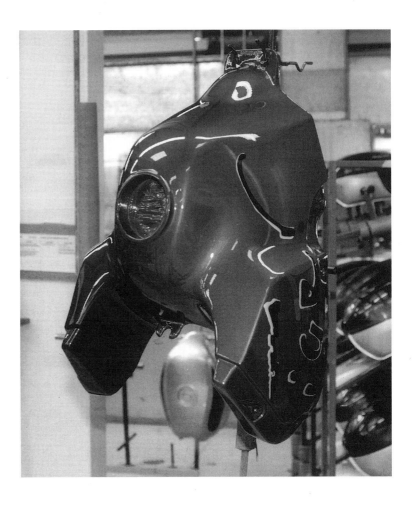

they use the wet-on-wet method, implying that the primer is not allowed to dry before the next coat is applied. This can lead to the orange-peel texture, but a skilled sprayer will have the technique and dexterity to overcome it. John Bradley believes the motorcycle buyer is more critical of the bike's finish; after all, there is a lot less panelling on a bike compared with a car, so it has to be right – and right first time, as they cannot afford to have people rectifying mistakes as the panels come off the line.

The last of the paint booths is for a final clear coat to be applied, and the painted panels then proceed on their way to the oven to be baked, still on their pegs. A blast of hot air greets them at the entrance to the oven – not so much a tunnel, as a rectangular box in which the track turns back on itself, a format dictated by considerations of space. A line of freshly painted panels goes in on one side, while fresh stoved ones emerge on the other. In the dark cavern, the temperature is an uncomfortable 158°F (70°C), but it is not *so* hot as to prevent operators from going in to reset thermostats if a temperature imbalance occurs. Unlike the rest of the plant where the extractors are in the walls, those of the paint oven had to be in the roof as a matter of convenience.

Outside the oven, the panels pass the track's tensioner unit, where they are checked for any dirt specks, then they are set upon by the polishers – there are two sets of polishers to each line. The team leader marks up any areas where he feels extra attention is required. Paradoxically, the less attention the panel receives, the better, as too much fiddling causes blemishes. In another booth, tank badges are fitted to the Thunderbirds and Adventurers, a job taken from the Assembly line because it is more related to the cosmetic world of the Paint shop. The finished panels are fed back into blue trolleys to await transit to the Assembly line or Stores. In a bin to one side lie a handful of discarded panels, rejected because of some irredeemable scar. It would be too time-consuming to put these items through the preparation process again, so they are junked. Some time ago a scrap-yard was involved in illicit sales of these items at autojumbles, and so dud panels are now hacked about by a chainsaw before they are allowed to leave the factory to prevent any chance of their being used again.

Special Effects

The sparkling twin-coloured effect is achieved on tanks by applying a silver base coat, and then overspraying the actual colour required; the silver shines through. Silver infill is achieved by careful masking; this is done in a central booth, where decals are also applied. Sometimes tanks are taken off their pegs for ease of masking up,

Panels for painting, such as these Tiger headlight surrounds, are mounted on pegs, on which they complete their trip through the various paint shop cubicles and oven.

(Below)
An air tool is used to fix the distinctive Triumph badge to the Thunderbird tank.

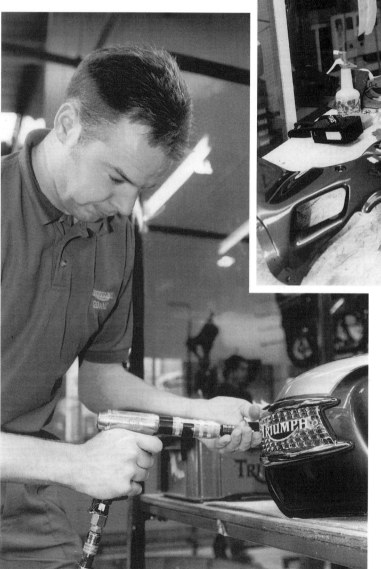

(Above) *Midway through the paint shop process, the Tiger's distinctive logo is applied to the fairing panels and tank as a number of separate transfers. They go on to be sealed with a coat of lacquer.*

and much care is needed as the main colour is still wet at this stage. Any bleed-over is carefully removed with a solvent rag. We watched as the Tiger's distinctive logo was applied to the panels: the self-adhesive transfer comes in several sections, made by Super Signs, and each cut exactly to fit the apertures in the panel, and carefully fitted by hand. Because there is no defining contour on the tank, a finished panel is offered up to locate the decal on the tank. They line up perfectly – so for those looking at a used bike, if the decals don't match accurately, it must have been crash repaired.

The coachlines on the classic models are difficult to achieve and warrant special treatment, and are still done by hand in the traditional way by one man, Gary Devine. Aged thirty-six, he is the third generation of his family to be a Triumph employee; he was at Meriden in the 1970s, and just before the closure, he was doing what he does now:

Some jobs just can't be automated. Gary Devine, a third generation Triumph employee, paints coachlines freehand on the classic bikes' tanks and mudguards – and there's not a roll of masking tape to be seen.

painting coachlines on tanks. Although times and circumstances change, for Gary, the materials he uses remain much the same – and these have had their problems: 'The paint they recommend us to use does not actually stick – that's the kind normal-ly used to paint coachlines on trucks and buses. They're all right if you don't want to clear-coat over it – but we do, unfortunate-ly, and you can't get the lacquer to stick on top of it. So ours is specially formulated for us by our regular paint manufacturer.' The

Gary Devine mixes his own pigments for the gold coachlines, and uses special brushes with long bristles and cut-down handles.

An assortment of freshly painted Sprint, Thunderbird and Trident fuel tanks sit on racks before going off to assembly.

coachlines are dry enough to lacquer over in about ten minutes, like the regular base coat. Different paints give different problems: the black they use is quite good because it covers in one go, whereas Gary has to go over the gold lines twice – thus demanding twice as much concentration because of course he then has to follow his first line exactly. With studied gaze he paints one side, then the other, by which time the first line is dry enough for a second coat. Whereas the black comes ready made, Gary has to mix the gold pigment first with lacquer, then with thinners to get the right consistency. It's a job not without its ironies: 'We actually had a Trident tank returned to us by the warranty department because the customer complained he could see brush marks in the gold line,' said Gary. 'We just laughed and said "Yes, that would be right!"' Apparently the company had recently tried at least ten painters so as to take some of the pressure off Gary, but only one or two had the ability to do the coachlines; on the other hand, Gary also does spraying and preparation with the best of them. For coachlining he uses special long-bristled brushes called swordliners. He cuts the handles down so they fit exactly between his finger and thumb, and keeps the bristles oiled so they remain supple and smooth. I asked him what he considered were the special qualities needed to do coachlining: 'It's not just a steady hand, what you really need is a good eye. What you're doing is just following a line, although there's a bit of an artistic flair to it, I suppose!' Unlike at Harley-Davidson, a roller could not be used to paint Triumph coachlines because it couldn't negotiate the lip at the bottom of the tank. However, the shadow of automation may yet fall on the hand-painted coachline, simply because it is so time-consuming to do; in fact Triumph's cosmetic advisers may be asked to re-think the Thunderbird livery so that a faster system may be implemented.

THE ASSEMBLY LINE

The Assembly area is virtually self-contained, and so small it is easily comprehensible to the visitor; almost a cottage industry. It is organized in teams: the engine line in two groups, the chassis line in three, then there is the body line, and a test and rectification area at the end. There are thus seven team leaders; these are under the guidance of one supervisor, and each team comprises seven operators.

Eighty bikes a day are assembled here, and it takes just five-and-a-half hours to assemble one machine from nuts and bolts. Because of the moving conveyors, each person is allowed six minutes and twenty seconds per bike to perform his or her task. This is actually quite generous compared with the scant one minute allowed at Nissan. Each team has an emergency track-stop button to bring everything to a halt in case of an emergency, and individual workers also have access to a help button to call on the assistance of the team leader if required. The track will only be stopped as a last resort.

It is helpful to visualize the assembly department as a square plan, with conveyors around three sides of the square. There are two conveyors along side one, the first for the engine assembly, ending in the cold-test machine; then the engine joins the frame, and this process takes place on the second conveyor. On side two of the square, the bike frames are suspended on an aerial conveyer which carries them along as components are fitted. They turn the corner into the third side of the square, and here the fairings are fitted. A final conveyor takes the nearly finished machines along to the end of the line, from where they will be offloaded onto the platform for engine and emissions testing. After this comes the rolling road, and this is notionally the fourth side of the square.

The Assembly section in particular is based on the Japanese principle, the work shared between six teams. The engines begin life in the skilled hands of team 1, who start by selecting components from the bins placed on the outside of the line.

A bike about to be assembled is preceded by its build sheet: this gives its factory order number, the model, colour and country of destination, and lists its full specification. This ticket accompanies the bike all the way round the Assembly department to packing stage. Whatever the model, all the various details appear on a screen monitor. As it is programmed in, the build cards come out in sequences of ten. It is a very neat system, although more easily appreciated when viewed on site. To take a random example, in engine line 1 the builder would identify number 7 as a T409 Tiger to be built to A1 spec, which gives its particular details; or it may be an RC T309, which is a UK market Adventurer, whose A1 spec may call for flat-top pistons and long-stroke conrods. All cranks and crankcases, mains and ends have bar-codes on them, and there are two grades of conrod, either A or B, and the number is the weight of the conrod. There is a 3g difference between weights one-to-ten on the grading scale. All this is tied in with the designated engine number, and the latter, together with bar-codes for crank and crankcase, gives the colour codes for ends and mains. The shells are in colour-coded shelves, and they are selected and placed on the track in the correct order for assembly. All this information is recorded on the build ticket as well.

The components are prepared and washed prior to build, all the while moving steadily towards the assembly line. For instance, the crankcase halves arrive straight from the Machine shop: they will have been standing in a stillage for maybe a day, in pairs – and numbered thus, say BC47 and BC47 – and they will be placed in

On the engine assembly line, one of the first tasks is to install cranks and big-end shells.

another crankcase wash by line 1. This is a three-minute process in which the components are washed twice, then dried with a hot air dryer and a vacuum dryer, thus ensuring that all the blind holes and internal bores are bone dry. Cranks, liners and conrods receive similar treatment in a separate wash compartment.

Meanwhile, balance shafts have their gears pressed on. The base flange of the crankcase used to be sealed with Hylamar compound, but this was dropped a couple of years ago because the machining is now so exact that a sealant is not necessary, and a clean fit is obtained without it. The engine builders employ a double-check system: to ensure the correct final torque setting for concealed retainers – for example, a bolt hidden inside the engine – the operator will mark it with a green felt-tip pen to show he has fitted it, and also to indicate that it has had a final torque setting. When it goes down to the next station, the operator looks for the green mark, and he will overcheck it with a blue felt-tip pen.

On the conveyor, the top crankcase half sits in a jig, and as it moves along, the internals are installed. Cylinder liners, pistons and conrods have been made into a smaller sub-assembly. Triumph engines use wet liners – which make for ease of assembly as well as replacement if ever a rebore should be required – and these are pushed in and clamped into position in the top crankcase half, using an air tool. Then the jig holding the crankcase half is rotated through 180 degrees, and the crankshaft is carefully fitted.

The crankcase then reaches the second stage on the line, where the ready prepared gear cluster and clutch are installed. Thus within a mere six feet from the beginning of the line, the two crankcase halves are together and it is looking like a finished engine; something like half-an-hour has elapsed.

With gear clusters installed, crankshaft pulleys are located with the ubiquitous air tools which hang like jungle creepers throughout the assembly area.

*Camshafts are placed in the
cylinder head; by now the engine is
moving towards completion.*

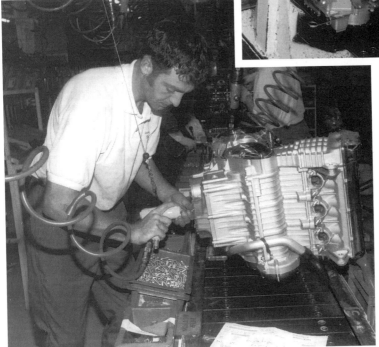

*Engine line 1 is equipped with
special jigs and hoists so that
the engine can be worked on
from any angle.*

A complete engine is readied for the cold engine test; it is filled with oil and linked to the machine on the right, where it is driven but not fired up. This establishes that compression and voltage are satisfactory.

In the early days the engine number was literally cast onto the crankcase; nowadays it is stamped on by dot matrix system, which is virtually foolproof as far as forgery is concerned. Next come the carburettors, generators, starter motors and the wiring loom. Should any problems be discovered with an engine they can be rectified at the end of section one. Any minor problems – and there are very, very few – can be dealt with on the line, provided no swarf is created.

Cold Test

Before they go any further, the completed engines are filled with hot oil – which is thinner and thus more searching, and also cuts down frictional resistance – and are plumbed in to the cold engine test. The machine which carries out this test is housed in a white rectangular container, and drives each engine from the gearbox sprocket without it having to be fired up (hence 'cold' test); an engine being run in this way emits a peculiar hollow sound. The machine can be checking three engines at once, and achieves the following: it reveals any oil leaks or vibrations; it shows whether the clutch mechanism is working properly, also that gear selection is operating properly as it goes up and down through the gears; it checks torque output from the gears, oil pressure, compression, starter motor function and generator output. The cold test facility itself is checked every six months to ensure that the calibrations remain accurate.

It is virtually certain that no faulty engine will get beyond this stage. So providing all is well, the oil is drained away and the engine moves along to the second stage, and into the care of chassis teams 1 and 2.

Engine Meets Chassis

This is where the engine joins the chassis-frame. The engines are mounted on special stands on a roller conveyor, and the frames are made ready, with their numbers stamped on: then with a certain amount of physical effort, they are dropped on over the top of the engine. There are two bolt fixings on the front of the engine, one on each side on top of the gearbox, and the swinging-arm is pinned in place at the lowest point of the frame. The rear suspension, swinging-arms and rear mudguards are prepared in advance for each up-coming bike by chassis team 3, who are located just beyond the

assembly line, and are then slotted into place. The new T595 and T509 alloy frames are easier to comprehend; they have eight mounting points for the engine, four on either side. The chassis 1 team leader, Rob Miller, describes the differences in the back-bone chassis frames:

We try to work as much as possible on a sequence-fed system, so trolleys come supplied with frames from the powder-coating booth. At the moment they come in batches for either three- or four-cylinder bikes, but in fact it would be better if they came sequence-fed in the right order for the day's

Anatomy of a Triumph revealed: the bare bones of the powertrain, together with chassis spine, seat frame, monoshock and double-sided swing-arm are clearly visible.

As a T595 reaches the point where engine line meets chassis line 1, two of the aluminium alloy frame's eight engine mountings are tightened.

production – that would save time as well as space. They are all produced in the same area, so a revision to the system would encourage them not to produce in such large batches, because ideally they should only produce what we want to use. There's no point the welding shop or the plating shop producing fifty sets of 900 downpipes if we only need thirty. We produce seventy-two bikes a day, so if they get into the habit of sequence-feeding, they'll produce what we actually need, and not be wasting their time.

The black-coated frames are the Trident and Tiger derivatives, and the grey frames are for the Trophy and Sprint. The Thunderbird and Adventurer look very similar, but weight balance is different for the single-seater bike. Because the Thunderbird may carry a passenger, and thus more weight towards the rear of the bike, the frame

119

weight is actually biased further forward than on the Adventurer. Being a trail bike, the Tiger is higher at the front and back, and seating position and balance are different from the Trident, so there are slight differences in the frame all the way through. Similarly, the Trophy frame is different from the Sprint, mainly in the strengthening plate added to the Trophy to support its fitted luggage panniers. The Sprint chassis is bare under the rear seat area, and it is only really towards the back end that there are differences. You really have to work on the chassis areas to appreciate those differences.

The Tiger, Trident, Sprint and Trophy frames arrive at Chassis 1 ready for components to be bolted on, with no further sub-assemblies to take into account.

After the swinging arm has been joined onto the chassis frame, the spark plugs are screwed in, the plug leads fitted, and the wiring harness put in place, all 40ft (12m) of it clipped to the frame. At each stage an operator checks that the bolts have actually been torqued up, and also makes sure that the engine number matches the chassis number on the build-ticket. The main airbox and the expansion tank for the coolant goes on, along with the main downpipe section of the exhaust system.

There are obvious differences in the exhausts: bright chrome ones go on the RT and RC classic models, while untreated, stainless steel pipes go on Trophy derivatives – because it is a fully faired bike there is no need for shiny exhaust headers because nobody will see them. The black-chromed downpipes are for the Tiger enduro, the Trident and the Sprint. All pipes start off being stainless steel, whatever their ultimate aesthetic treatment.

As the frame-engine assembly gets to the end of this short track, it meets the overhead orange-coloured conveyor and comes under the control of Chassis 2. The frame is hooked onto cradles which carry it along, while it collects suspension, wheels, cooling system, downpipes and instruments, by courtesy of teams 3 and 4. Wire wheel rims are made by Akront in Spain, although hubs are British made, and the stainless steel

Chassis 2 team leader, Stuart Reader, fits a Thunderbird rear disc. Tyres are fitted and wheels are balanced in an area at the corner of the chassis lines.

A consignment of 17 × 3in Tiger rear wheels has arrived in the stores. Stainless steel spokes will be fitted by the Leicestershire-based Central Wheel Company.

(Below)
Some Avon 160/80 T16 tyres are selected from the stores for fitting to Thunderbird and Adventurer rears.

spokes are fitted by the Central Wheel Company at Coalville. Towards the end of this section, coolant is added, and the bikes pass on to team 5: here, switchgear is fitted, more instruments go on, and the hydraulic systems – brake and clutch fluid reservoirs – are installed.

They then turn the corner onto the body line, the third leg of the Assembly facility, where hydraulic fluids are bled through. In a small ante-room off to the left is the carburettor test area where carbs are checked, direct from Mikuni. They are already set up to a reasonably high standard, and after fitting and plumbing in, the mule three- and four-cylinder engines are run 'on the bench' and the carbs tuned to check that mixture settings and exhaust emissions are exactly right. The carbs are nearly always acceptable for the UK market when they arrive, but further fine tuning is needed to satisfy the Australian and Californian markets.

(Above) *To the side of the assembly line there is a small room dedicated to carburettor testing: here, the team leader, Karl Orton, sets up a trio on a triple.*

A rack of chrome air-box covers is trolleyed from stores to the assembly shop.

The operator reads off data on the computer screen, and CO emissions are left at 3 per cent on British bikes and 1 per cent on US bikes. Carbs on Swiss bikes are the most restricted of all, with just a quarter of the inlet tract available for air intake, so severe is the environmental legislation. Understandably this has a detrimental effect on performance, and in practice owners are said to de-restrict their machines once in the country. It happens over here with the restricted grey import 400cc Japanese race-reps too. It is another reason why big-engined bikes are popular in countries such as Switzerland, because cubic capacity can redress the balance to a certain extent.

Once set up, the carbs are placed on racks in the right sequence to meet their intended bike as it comes down the line. It follows that the motor must be correctly set up from this point onwards, so an exhaust gas analysis is not necessary after the rolling road test.

This is the body line, and they work two to a bike, around ten people in all. The bikes receive their fairings here; the Adventurers and Thunderbirds get their rear mudguards and wheel covers pop-rivetted on; while the Trophys, Tigers and Daytonas receive their

On Chassis line 5, Lance Chard fits an enduro with its side panels.

(Above) *Fettling an Adventurer – note the single seat frame – on Chassis line 5.*

Jobs such as fitting the rear lights and pop-rivetting the wheel cover on the back mudguard of this Thunderbird are carried out beside Chassis line 5.

A Trident fuel tank is fitted by Richard Jakeman as the bike nears the end of the assembly line.

infill panels, fairings and front mudguards. The Sprint, for instance, has a three-piece cockpit fairing, the sections sprayed separately in the paint shop; they are placed into the jig for fibreglass panels beside the track and are welded together with an ultra-sonic tool before being fitted to the bike on the conveyer. A new line in moulded fibreglass luggage was being set up on one of my visits, with two young women making Trophy panniers by the side of the track. Fuel tanks are installed, and all the remaining electrical components are fitted at this stage, namely lights, indicators and igniters. The bikes are now just yards away from the end of the production line.

Towards the end of 1996, Triumph began producing its own luggage in-house. In an area at the rear of Chassis line 4, two members of the workforce make up panniers.

RECTIFICATION

As the complete bikes get to the end of the line, some four-and-a-half hours from the beginning of engine line 1, they are claimed by Rectification, where checking begins in earnest. The quality control team here is encouraged to be aggressive in seeking out errors or potential problems and the bikes are subjected to a sixty-five area check, with perhaps six points per area; thus after road testing, every bike will have had 200 aspects checked. Triumph, I was told, does not want to burden its dealers with problems, let alone its customers.

A special saddle incorporating a battery is connected up to each machine, and the bikes are filled up with fresh oil, the coolant level checked, and with two litres of fuel on board, started up for the first time and run up to operating temperatures. At this point large wall-mounted fans cut in. While this is going on the engineers are checking panel-fit, electrical functions, connections and so on.

ROLLING ROAD

When all appears to be in order, the bikes are ridden individually by the in-house test rider into the rolling road booth where each one is subjected to a fifteen-point check-up. There are two sets of rollers – predictably one for the front and one for the back – and

An Adventurer is checked for exhaust emissions in the rectification department, with a pair of Sprints in the background. Carbon monoxide emissions are left at 3 per cent on home market bikes.

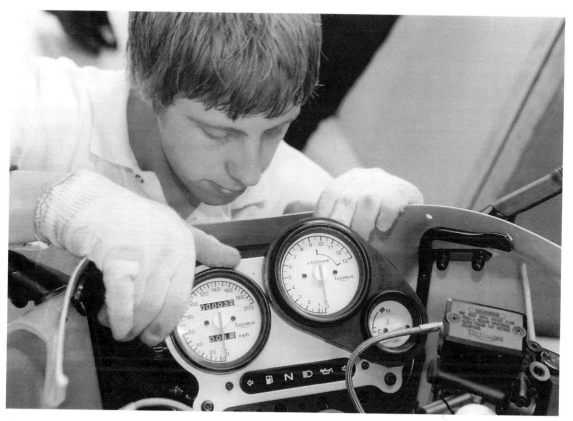

Further checks are made on finished bikes in rectification: the dial alignment on a 1996 Daytona is adjusted by Greg Page.

the bikes are taken up to 78mph (125.5kph), one wheel at a time. At this speed the test rider brakes heavily down to zero, first with the front brake and again with the rear; this will show up any deficiency, with brakes or wheels buckled or out of balance. Clutch and gear operation come under scrutiny, and then finally the rear rollers become the dynomometer, testing the power output of the engine. Clearly these engines have not been run in, so they are only taken up to 16bhp in the case of the classic models, the Tiger and Trident to 23bhp, and the rest up to 29bhp. Considering the Super III

produces 107bhp at the gearbox sprocket, this is very mild, approximating 78mph (125.5kph); however, it is quite adequate for evaluation.

Fifteen minutes later the bike has completed the rolling road test, and comes down a ramp to the Test and Rectification area, where the cut-out switches are checked. Then the oil is drained out and recycled, to be junked after three days. Final inspection weeds out any machine with paint blemishes, fluid leaks: even the minutest detail is checked yet again. Within the rectangle formed by the assembly lines, there are a

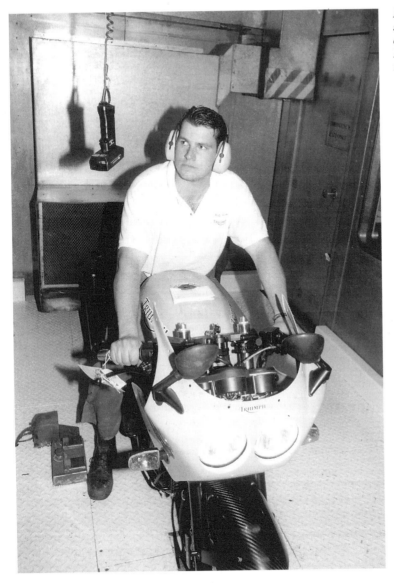

In-house test rider Rob Cole studies the telemetry gauges as he puts a mid-1996 Super III through its paces on the rolling road.

couple of control booths where supervisors pore over screens and production schedules. There is also an area where fully-built bikes are prepared for shows, or they might come under evaluation by the R & D team, or press bikes might be in for servicing and refettling.

Once finished, the bikes are signed off, and are ready for Dispatch.

DISPATCH

After assembly, and once the test procedure has been accomplished, the new machines go on to the Dispatch department. The crating process is very thorough, and is more or less the same whether a bike is going just five miles down the road to the Windy Corner

(Above) *After draining oil and fuel, Darren O'Regan and Ian Lamb prepare to hoist a Thunderbird onto the track where it will be crated up prior to dispatch.*

All bikes are strapped down in wooden crates whatever their destination. Here one is being made for a 1996 Daytona by Dean Huckle using a compressed air hammer.

Packing cases are fork-lifted into bays in Dispatch to await transit to dealerships.

dealership at Barnwell or to South Africa. However, bikes for export are given more compact cases than those for the UK market, in order to fit in to the shipping containers.

On most models the bars are loosened and pushed in, but the classic models are too wide for the crate and have their taken off for transit. The bike goes on a roller conveyor, and a wooden case is built up round it by a small team of joiners, one to a bike, using compressed air hammers to nail up the wooden sides and battens. The bike is firmly strapped down so that it can't move, and is comprehensively Waxoyled. The crate is then clad in a cardboard box, and goes to join others by the side of the lofty building to await transit. The various destinations inked on the sides of the boxes have their individual codes: US for the States, and UC for California cases, F for France, J for Japan, and so on, just as you would expect. The final act before they leave the factory gates is to fork-lift them on pallets onto trucks backed up to the loading bay.

6 Sales and Marketing

PTo sell bikes means creating a high profile, and one of the main problems facing Triumph and its sales people is overcoming public ignorance of the fact that the bikes are still in production. Almost every outing on a modern Triumph is greeted at some point with the question 'Do they still make them, then?'. Promotions such as the Speed Triple Challenge series help of course, although these are preaching to the knowledgeable if not the converted. It also helps if Triumphs are coveted by the rich and famous. Lord Lichfield has a 900 Daytona, as do Daniel Day-Lewis and Hugh Laurie. Mark Knopfler rides a 1200 Daytona and Strangler Jean-Jaques Burnel favours a Thunderbird. Another rock musician, Dave Stewart, rides Triumph and Bruce Springsteen has a bike on either coast; there was the Meatloaf video, too. And it helps if Triumphs are seen on the silver screen, not merely classic bikes, such as in Jean-Claud van Damme's Tiger antics in *Nowhere to Run*, but *Bay Watch*'s Pamela Anderson strutting her stuff as the eponymous *Barb Wire*. Here the statuesque proprietor of the Hammerhead saloon cruises the anarchic urban wastelands of the 21st Century Steel Harbour on her Thunderbird, climaxing astride her Tiger like a mediaeval knight in a jousting contest. I gather she actually bought the bikes for the film herself, and good for her. One wonders just how many in the cinema audiences recognized the bikes as Triumphs. Likewise the zany cookery duo Jennifer Paterson and Clarissa Dickson

Wright were seen bumbling about in the BBC television series *Two Fat Ladies*, aboard their modern Thunderbird and classic Watsonian combination. Sadly, probably only the cognoscente will recognize the bikes, and it won't mean a thing to the casual viewer. Therefore the mission to inform people must continue.

IN-HOUSE PROFESSIONAL

Triumph's sales and marketing manager is Bruno Tagliaferri, an amazingly relaxed and accommodating professional, who joined the firm in 1989. That was six months before the first bike was produced, and although the production line was in place, there was no sales distribution system. Bruno had the considerable experience of having been in sales and marketing at Honda for twelve years, to put Triumph back on its feet: he made a big decision going to the company when the renaissance was in its infancy, and there were certainly a few anxious times as sales fluctuated. The first two years were the most critical. Bruno set up a thirty-five dealer network which was operational by March 1991, and to an extent it is still expanding. There are about fifty-five UK dealers now, with dealerships in thirty-one countries worldwide.

'We don't expect the network to grow much more, because we're a specialized product and people will readily travel twenty-five miles to see a Triumph. In turn, we get a lot back from the dealers; they get a good territory and a good product, and there is a good spread nationally,' he said.

It is rare to have to travel more than 40 miles (64km) to get to a Triumph dealer, and if you do, it is almost certainly because geographically it is a barren area. I have relatives near Carlisle, and noted that there is no Triumph dealer in Cumbria; however, apparently people will go to Newcastle or Lancashire for their Triumphs. I pointed out to Bruno that there are both Honda and Kawasaki dealers side by side in Carlisle, and at one point in 1996 they seemed to be almost overflowing with brand-new CBR 600s.

'That proves my point,' said Bruno, 'because the main dealers in the big cities have hardly any. We would sell only a dozen or so Triumphs a year in Carlisle, so it would not be worth our while to have a solus dealer there.'

Promotion is relatively low key, and relies largely on dealers advertising in the motorcycle press; there has also been television advertising in Germany and France. The Speed Triple Challenge is probably the most prominent activity in which the company is involved. There is also the articulated mobile shop, seen first at the 1996 Grand Prix at Donington. Bruno operates with just himself and two others, and there are three people in overseas sales, with an export sales and marketing manager. This is typical of the John Bloor philosophy: a skeleton staff, with projects prioritized.

That briefly sums up the factory sales side of things: those who want a new bike go to a specialist dealer. But what about buying a used Triumph? It might be possible to strike a cheaper deal by getting one privately, and if the service record is complete, or you know the seller, that might be the way to go. On balance though, my feeling about buying secondhand is that a buyer will have far better security from a specialist dealer who will pro-

vide warranty and service back-up. It might be possible to buy a bike several hundred pounds cheaper privately, but there will be no certainty as to its reliability, notwithstanding a full service record. I asked Barry Lynes, the manager at Ling's Watton branch what to look for if buying a secondhand Triumph, and he replied confidently:

> All bikes originally came with a two-year warranty, so any problems would have been sorted during that period. Initially there were a few with duff fork seals, but once they were dealt with, there wouldn't be any more trouble. Any used bike bought from a Triumph dealer automatically comes with a one-year warranty and RAC cover.

Having suffered from not having this cover with my CBR, I can only endorse it as being the way to go.

THE RETAILER'S VIEW

Ling's principal at its Ipswich showroom is Paul Barkshire, and he had plenty to say regarding the sale of Triumphs:

> The perception is that you have to give discounts to sell bikes. Now that may be true of Hondas, where people say if you don't give me a deal, you don't sell the bike. We ran out of Hondas in summer 1996, and the company was caught out – it couldn't react fast enough and accordingly we hadn't any new Hondas to sell. But with Triumph it's a different matter. If we ring them up and say, 'We're down to our last bike, have you got a couple to tide us over?' they're here within ten days. There is a limitation though, because towards the end of the model year, production has gone over to the new models for the coming year, so it does call for careful stock control and for sorting out forward

Paul Barkshire, principal of Ling's Ipswich branch, finds traditional Harley-Davidson and Moto Guzzi riders trading in their machines for Thunderbirds.

orders by September. Otherwise you've got very little chance of getting any more bikes. But they won't saturate the market either, and that has a double-edged effect. First, it protects the customer, and second, it protects the price to the dealer, because if you're down to a few bikes and you know there's not going to be any more, then you don't have to discount. There are fifty-three dealers nationwide and they all know the score.

At one stage about two years ago *MCN* stated that Triumphs were holding stronger residual market values than Harley-Davidson. Said Paul:

People buy Harley-Davidsons not necessarily for the ride or the looks, but because they know they will sell at a profit. And there's a shortage of used Triumphs. While we have statistics on new sales, nobody has stats on used bikes. There is a big demand for used Triumphs. John Bloor has a tremendous reputation for detail, for getting it right, and the bikes deserve that reputation.

It wasn't always sweetness and light, though. When Triumph started producing bikes again there were plenty of critics.

We British are a strange nation, and we love to shoot down anybody who appears to be getting on. So Triumph never pushes us, although of course there is an underlying agenda for sales successes. But the company has never stressed it. As long as they know you're a good dealership and you're working hard, which they know from the sales, you're given all the support you could wish for. Our sales promotion majored on the fact that the bikes were British-made. We weren't focused on the actual deal, the immediate sale; we realized there was a longer scenario, and we worked hard at the sales targets. If there was a problem, Triumph would offer any assistance they could to get the dealer out of it.

That isn't necessarily the case throughout the motorcycle industry, however. 'Naming no names,' said Paul, 'but if you were to ring up a certain Japanese company you'd invariably find they were in meetings. But ring Triumph, and you'll always get through to the person you want.' I remarked that the elusive Mr Bloor is a different matter. 'Well, he's a difficult man to get hold of. I've an idea he's actually been in my franchise and not let it be known,' said Paul. 'But you don't need to talk to him because the supervisory staff there can answer the majority of questions.'

I still wanted to quantify sales volumes, new against secondhand. Said Paul:

We've been with Honda for nearly thirty-eight years; we were 100 per cent Japanese.

Then five years ago Triumph reappeared, and we were in from day one. It's difficult to quantify on a week-by-week basis, but whereas some weeks we might not sell a single Honda, we'll sell half-a-dozen Triumphs. Supply problems also affect the stats, but sale for sale, we're probably selling 45 per cent Triumphs to 55 per cent Hondas, and you have to bear in mind that the Honda range is far broader than Triumph's – even a moped counts as a motorcycle sale. So for Triumphs to represent nearly half our sales is really quite phenomenal.

Despite the gloomy predictions a few years ago about legislation seeing off the big bike market, Paul Barkshire is confident about the future:

I can see the market for big bikes just growing and growing. Some people asked why I wasn't keen to push the commuter market. Fine in the city maybe, but where are all the commuters in this area? Apart from Ipswich our catchment is largely rural. You just have to weigh up the stats. So my focus was on the brand-new company and after-sales service, with an eye on the future. We were selling to local people first and developing the business after that.

It has worked, too. From the small Norfolk town of Watton (Ling's have branches in Ipswich, Harleston and Lowestoft as well) to East Anglia, Ling's now sells machines and parts nationwide. Paul again:

We have good customers in Scotland and Wales – people will travel. On the one hand there's the 'pile 'em high and sell 'em cheap' philosophy, but Triumph is not like that. They were aware that their fifty-four dealers were pretty much hands-on people, so that even as a branch manager, I could be out in the street adjusting somebody's

chain. It's the personal touch that Triumph people like. We are a service industry.

Most of the secondhand bikes in Ling's showroom in mid-1996 were Triumphs. That, argued Barkshire, proved the customer was getting such a good return on his bike that he was coming back for another one, and in turn, this established that there *is* a demand for used bikes too. But while Ling's now have confidence in every area of Triumph sales and service, there were worrying times. Explained Paul:

It was an unknown quantity; we didn't know what the market would stand. We had to debate what we should give for a motorcycle being traded in, and ask ourselves whether

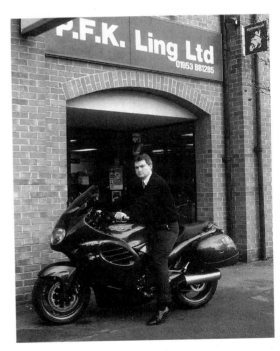

Managing Director Barry Lynes of Ling's of Watton astride a 1996-spec Trophy 900. Despite the onset of winter weather and Christmas, traditionally a slack period for bike sales, he sold eight machines in the first week of December 1996.

a Triumph that's maybe two or three years old would sell. It was something we had to gauge – and we were very quickly made aware of the public's perception of the bikes as an all-round fantastic piece of kit. Plus there was a full service back-up.

All secondhand bikes have a year's Triumph Care Warranty which is also linked to the dealer; in mid-1996 this was quite unique in motorcycling. This facility was instigated by Bruno Tagliaferri, who perceived that in order to win and consolidate a loyal Triumph ownership, the buyer of a used bike needed to be supported as well as the buyer of a brand new one. It was a ground-breaking move which probably upset the Japanese makers. But not only were riders looked after when they'd bought the bike, its acquisition was made easy through Triumph's low-rate finance, there was Triumph care insurance, plus a fourteen-day exchange plan on bikes bought from dealers.

TRIUMPH CLUBS

Facilities such as those identified above are all calculated to increase sales. In addition, Triumph puts on its own shows, it goes to the Isle of Man, and there is a new factory-organized owners' club. Perhaps understandably, there is some conflict here with the long-established Triumph club, which sees itself as the true representative of the marque. Until the dust settles there may have to be two Triumph clubs: one for the classic, Meriden-produced machines, and one for the modern Hinckley models. One disparity between the two sides is that many of the older bikes are mothballed, and quite rightly, strictly fair-weather rides, whereas the majority of new-model owners ride whenever they feel like it. There is a crossover, naturally, and the situation is not altogether polarized.

The factory-backed club is called RAT, an acronym for Riders' Association of Triumph – started at the beginning of 1997; it features the normal sort of club activity – weekends away to foreign parts, regional gatherings, rides to race meetings, as well as a quarterly magazine called *Torque* – all calculated to foster a strong Triumph following and to enable owners to get full use and enjoyment out of their machines. The company's dealer network is involved on the promotional side of RAT as well, being natural communication centres.

An important facet of Triumph's publicity is the factory tour, described earlier, which allows those with a keen interest in the marque and biking in general to see how they make them. In liaison with the factory, the tour groups are organized by the dealerships, and consist of twenty or so customers and their partners. For example, Ling's have also taken parties from the big Suffolk US air force bases such as Mildenhall and Lakenheath. 'We ride up with them, have lunch with them prior to going round the factory, and we're treated like one of the lads!' said Paul Barkshire.

Paul was sufficiently confident of Ling's future as a Triumph dealer – and by implication, the continuing success of Triumph – demonstrated by the opening of its new Ipswich showroom.

BUYER PROFILE

By and large, the typical Triumph owner is a mature individual. Prices of new and secondhand models are relatively high, so it has to be someone in work to be able to finance the purchase and maintenance of the machine. In the trade in general, licensing rules and insurance premiums make it prohibitive for youngsters to own Triumphs; theirs is clearly the province of sports 125s

The Thunderbird sells to a younger age range than Triumph expected: riders in their twenties as well as those in their thirties and forties are buying the classic-styled bikes.

and maybe 250s. Besides which, Triumphs are big capacity, relatively heavy machines.

Paul Barkshire points to the professional and semi-professional buyer, but believes Ling's clientele is somewhat at variance with the national trend, in that he has customers of twenty-five and thirty years old buying Thunderbirds and Adventurers, the sort of machine normally sought by an older rider. For the first three years of Hinckley production, Triumphs appealed to the older person, probably because the image was more conservative and you had to be of a certain age to remember the marque's Meriden heritage. Nationally, the average age of

the Triumph buyer has dropped to thirty, many of whom are riders coming back to motorcycling having had a family and its associated commitments, and for whom the principal requirement is reliability. I can state this from direct first-hand experience: the last thing you want when commuting 70 miles (113km) home on a dark winter's evening is to be pushing your lifeless machine down the hard shoulder; what was perhaps acceptable when you were sixteen is certainly not so when you are in the full flush of middle age. Triumphs appear to provide that kind of reliability. Says Paul:

> We have found that in a harder winter, the Japanese rider tends to disappear, up to 600 or 750cc, at any rate; whereas the Triumph owner is out there all year round.

Triumph riders, it seems, are doing a lot more miles than the average biker, including trips abroad. Triumph was at one time the only company to offer RAC Euro recovery as part of the two-year warranty package – normally this has to be ordered specially.

Four or five years ago, the sort of bikes being traded in against Triumphs were the Harley-Davidsons, BMWs and Moto Guzzis owned by people who had already gone against the grain in the Japanese-dominated marketplace. Triumphs were seen as individual, as well as locally made, relatively speaking. Proof that Triumph has got its sums right is that now, people are trading in FireBlades and VFR 750s against Daytonas and Trophys. On the other hand, there is no penalty to the dealer in the event of an order being cancelled. For example, Ling's found themselves carrying a couple of 1200 Trophys late on in the year, when it was clear they were unlikely to move. But 900 versions might, so Paul asked if they could swap. No problem: just a phone-call away.

Standing out above a sparkling array of Triumphs, the company's articulated roadshow sales and exhibition vehicle made its debut at the 1996 British Grand Prix meeting at Donington.

MERCHANDISING

The merchandising side is an essential part of any marketing operation, although it was slow to take off in more rural areas where there is always resistance to the new and trendy. Merchandise is exclusively the province of the dealers, apart from the factory's own promotions pantechnicon seen at race circuits, as detailed elsewhere. The Triumph-branded merchandise now available ranges from everyday motorcycle clothing to the sort of lifestyle accessories favoured by the rich and trendy. Any independent clothing store wishing to sell Triumph merchandise would have to buy its stock from one of the motorcycle dealerships. Unlike Harley-Davidson, who charge some £25k for the privilege of hanging one of its signs outside the shop, Triumph dealers enjoy the privilege of bearing the Hinckley logo for free. More significantly, the funds needed to take on a Harley merchandising operation are closer to £300k: a Harley dealer is obliged to carry over £50k-worth of parts, and £200k worth of clothing. Triumph, though, relies on its principal product to promote itself, and supplies its dealers with merchandise on a sales-related basis – although some in urban areas may match their Harley dealer colleagues' investment in clothing, such is the confidence in the marketing potential of the Triumph badge.

Ling's follows the majority and sees the clothing side as a second string activity, supporting its main business of selling and servicing bikes. 'You can't be blasé about it,' said Paul. 'To make a success of it you've got to be fairly well up on clothing as it is potentially big business with quite generous margins.' Triumph's merchandise is not cheap either, the company having elected to go for the better quality garments and products, with no compromises. The merchandising representative is available in support, even to the extent of giving evening talks at dealerships to interested parties.

OVERSEAS SALES

It is probably the visual impact of the new Daytona and Speed Triple which will cause greatest excitement – and improve brand awareness – and since the marque has a staunch following in the States, many riders will want a piece of the action. Indeed, the USA market is really two distinct markets, so specific is Californian legislation. However, as yet the States is virgin territory as far as the revitalized company is concerned, and promotion there has been low key because Triumph has not yet had the capacity to satisfy such a potentially large market.

Perhaps surprisingly, Triumph's biggest overseas market is Germany, which accounts for 45 per cent of sales so far, compared with 27 per cent which remain in the UK. From the outset in 1991, Germany was the main overseas customer. In the past there has always been a problem in satisfying demand from Germany, which has resulted in the vast majority of German buyers remaining loyal to BMW.

France is in third place as a buyer, with roughly 11 per cent, and although Triumphs are expensive in France, they still command a higher reputation than Italian models. Being cheaper, Japanese machines have the edge here. Joint fourth in Triumph export figures are Greece and Australia. One doesn't normally associate Greece with big bikes – more the other end of the market, in fact – but that is what the sales statistics show; while as regards 'down under', they buy more bikes per head than anywhere else in the world. However, Triumph expects that the US market will take off, and maybe in a year from now will have overtaken British sales volumes.

As in Sweden, Spanish buyers have a fondness for Harleys, and high prices for Triumphs make them less attractive than the Japanese bikes in the marketplace. The Japanese themselves remain loyal to their own makes – except when it comes to classic bikes: like the archaic Mini Cooper and Caterham Seven, they have a seemingly unquenchable thirst for British sporting classics, and the 1960s Triumphs are no

exception. They like Bonnevilles especially, and that excludes post-Hinckley models. Maybe the unique triple engine and the new machines will help sway the balance. Italy is rather the same: if it's not red and called a Ferrari or a Ducati, then they are just not interested.

Like the Americans, the Swiss are also traditionally environmentally conscious, and the limitations placed on a powerful warhorse such as a 1200 Daytona serve to emasculate its performance severely. Inlet tracts are restricted, for example, and igniter boxes are different; but they do buy a lot of Triumph spares in Switzerland.

Exports mean a great deal to Triumph, and bikes such as this Tiger and Speed Triple are crated and dispatched regularly to the company's thirty-one overseas dealerships.

7 Riding Experiences

My nearest Triumph dealer is P.F.K. Ling's of Watton, and they very kindly lent me a selection of Triumphs to compare. I rode them for a week at a time, which enabled me to get acclimatized to each one and evaluate its individual characteristics. The first one they had available was a Tiger. I remembered a book read back in 1970s called *Jupiter's Travels* in which Ted Simon rode an archaic Triumph around the world, and thought how much better he would have got on with a modern Tiger. Seeing Ewan McGregor and Charley Boorman struggle to extricate their R1150GS Adventurers from Mongolian mud in *Long Way Round*, I doubt I could haul a Tiger upright in similar circumstances. Mind you, I came close at Morston on the Norfolk coast!

The unmetalled tracks and mudflats of the north Norfolk coast provided the author with ideal conditions to test the Tiger's off-roading potential.

THE TIGER

On the morning I picked the Tiger up it was drizzling, and as I rode away from Watton towards Norwich, the heavens opened. As the rain bounced off my lid and in through the half-open visor, I kept telling myself I was lucky to be astride a Tiger rather than a Daytona. And that sentiment holds true, because this model is exceptionally controllable: on the slippery road surface, its balance was exactly right to cope with any twitches, such as an over-enthusiastic take-off from a set of traffic lights. You sit up high – the bars are higher than a Trident or a Sprint – and this alone imparts a feeling of control. Although the centre of gravity seems higher than a regular machine, it still felt comfortable leaning in corners, and the more confident I got with it, the further it was possible to go down. I was told by someone at the factory that it is actually possible to scrape the passenger foot-pegs, but inspired though I became, I never got down that far.

Like Range Rovers in Chelsea, many enduros may hardly ever get a taste of the rough stuff; but paradoxically, these bikes are very good in an urban environment, because being higher up, you can see gaps in traffic much more easily. And the Tiger's long-travel enduro suspension makes it ideal for riding on our pot-holed, speed-humped city roads too. A disadvantage has to be the wind buffeting you get as you reach speeds of 70 and 80mph (110–125kph), especially if it is a head wind, so you either slow down or go as flat as possible on the tank – and given its enduro riding position, this is not a natural posture. Detuned 900 it may be, but it is a very powerful bike, so keen acceleration and high cruising speeds are easily achieved. On the other hand, you can go as slowly as you like without feeling absurd, which is difficult to do on a CBR, for instance. If touring, you wouldn't want to go flat out to catch a ferry on a Tiger, whereas you certainly wouldn't mind on a Trophy if you had to. On the Tiger you can ride in a relaxed way, just pottering along, which I have never found agreeable with the CBR. 'Horses for courses', naturally, and it comes into its own in another context – the one it was designed for: contrary to what some of the press has said about the Tiger, in mild off-roading conditions this bike is just fantastic. It soaks up the rough terrain of the farm track and green lane variety, and it is possible to go surprisingly quickly along the kind of unmade tracks to be found along the north Norfolk coast. Again, you probably wouldn't want to go quickly, but it's interesting as well as thrilling to find out that you can!

There are two things which make handling the Tiger a bit tricky. One is its height. I am over 6ft tall, but even so I found it took a fair kick to get astride it. The other thing is that it is a relatively heavy bike, at 460lb (209kg), which I discovered nearly to my cost: while playing in the muddy oozes of Moreston creek I almost foundered. Getting more and more bogged down, I had to try and turn round, and with the rapidly filling channel on one side and what appeared to be a trench of soft sediment between me and the dyke, I opted for a stony area in the direction of the creek which promised firmer going. More by luck than good judgement, I managed to maintain traction and find a route through the sticky grey mire without toppling over or getting bogged down. Bike and rider emerged, covered in cloying mud, but none the worse for wear. Few conventional machines could have coped – but then, maybe you would only consider going to such a place with an enduro like the Tiger. By now I loved the big black beast, and made all sorts of mental promises to a variety of potential financiers.

All the controls fell easily to hand, and I soon became familiar with their position

The Tiger is a tall, heavy machine to haul around in the rough, but nevertheless a capable performer off the beaten track.

and actuation. Mirrors were awkward, and always required a certain amount of fiddling with to get a good compromise position, as riding posture shifted according to speed – being crouched on the tank – or if growing tired and slumping on a long run: if you can't see the mirrors any more it must be time to take a break.

The Tiger's overall design has been well thought out, from the stainless steel cans with their heat shrouds tucked up high under the seat, to the headlight fairing and plastic pouches around the hand-grips. There are also one or two excellent safety measures built in: for instance, it will simply stall if you try to start it with the stand down, and if you forget to put it in neutral without the clutch in.

Triumph's enduro is certainly worthy of the name, although it is undeniably too

heavy and unwieldy for the sort of antics a hardened trailer might indulge in – come off, and not only would it be a heavy machine to right again, but that tasty paint scheme will have suffered, too. But then, an out-and-out trailie such as KTM's 609cc single-cylinder LC4 Rallye could never cruise comfortably across Europe two-up with luggage, and then take off into the wilderness. Fitting a pair of off-road tyres to a Tiger's wire-spoke wheels would instantly transform its ability in the rough stuff anyway, although it would probably shred a set of knobblies in no time on the road.

Funnily enough, big trail bikes aren't as popular in the UK as they are, say, in France, in spite of the craze here for four-wheel-drive off-roaders which peaked a couple of years ago. Better known machines such as Honda's Paris-Dakar replica XRV750 Africa Twin, and the smaller-engined and cheaper Aprilia Pegaso, BMW F650 Funduro, Yamaha XTZ 660 Ténéré and Suzuki DR800, have relatively low residual values. Others in this hunky dual-purpose segment include from Honda the TransAlp and Dominator, and the Tiger's chief rivals, BMW's R1100GS, and the slightly more powerful – and considerably cheaper – Cagiva Elefant 900. Of these two, the BMW is far better built.

Most of the motorcycle press believes the Tiger, while powerful, is too top-heavy ever to be wholly successful as an off-roader, and the Africa Twin usually comes top in tests. But since Honda UK sold a meagre 200 units of all three of their big trailies last year, making Tigers is hardly big business for Triumph.

THE ADVENTURER

Triumph's classic machines not only look the part, they ride like it too, an achievement which is praiseworthy as well as questionable: it is great that ability matches looks, but shouldn't handling have been sharpened up as well? Maybe the two things were always going to be incompatible.

The Adventurer which Ling's lent me had a dual seat option and very smart leather saddle bags, plus a natty clear-perspex windshield. Everywhere I went in urban areas it turned heads: when I was stopped for any reason, men of a certain age would come up to me and say things like 'Wow! Now that is a real motorcycle!' However, whereas on the CBR, or indeed other modern Triumphs, fellow riders give a fraternal nod in passing, I got no such acknowledgement when riding the Adventurer. Can its chrome-plated image really be so offensive to the modern biker? I hope not, because although it is a showpiece, it would be a wonderful bike to ride on a leisurely tour.

'Stay below 70mph (110kph),' advised Paul Barkshire. 'They don't like going much above that.' How right he was, because although the 900cc triple is a *blitzkrieg* performer, its limitations become all-too-suddenly apparent: hit 65mph (105kph) and you start to experience steering wobble – perhaps set off by the aerodynamics of the windshield – and you are very much aware of the turbulence created either by that screen again, or by the upright riding position – its bars are some way higher even than the Thunderbird. Triumph's classics certainly seem to pose some questions.

But what of its road manners? Do they match its classic looks, or is the razzle-dazzle a fake? That's perhaps the real surprise, to find yourself transported back to how these bikes behaved thirty years ago, because Triumph has endowed this retro stunner with retro handling as well. In the corners, I was aware of the front wheel's tendency to run wide – to understeer off, in fact – although it is easy enough to adjust your riding technique to suit. But is this a good thing, to deny progress in a sense, to embrace anew some of the less desirable traits of old bikes? Well, I think it's fine – honest, even, because it means the Adventurer isn't a fraudster, any more than a Yamaha V-Max or a Virago; it really *is* a classic bike, but because of its modern mechanicals, it's one with genuine attitude. In practical terms this also makes it an easy matter to do a ton, although the G-forces don't make for an enlightening experience. No, it's far better to see the Adventurer as a very comfortable leisure-touring machine, at its best on wide, open B roads, a bike which happens to have the turn of speed to get you out of trouble should you need it. And more to the point, it won't leave you marooned at the side of the road like a thirty-year old classic might. You could even indulge yourself aurally with this particular bike, as it was fitted with 'bad boy' cans, which gave free voice to the triple's bark.

The Adventurer isn't therefore the paradox I thought it might be – traditional looks with state-of-the-art running gear – and I came to the conclusion that its rider is someone who has nothing to prove except to indulge his taste in classic styling. Predictably it was aimed at the US market and, according to Ling's sales manager, was expected to be sold in fully finished trim,

that is, with all the extras. Ling's recognized the limitations of the retro market, however, ordering just three Adventurers in 1996.

I was surprised to discover how manoeuvrable it is, too. Those high bars and its low-slung centre of gravity make it easy to wheel around with the engine off, nor is there any sense of it being unwieldy when you are stationary at junctions or lights. Just don't try to do anything in a rush!

(Right) The Adventurer which Ling's lent the author really looked the part: it came fully equipped, with windshield, leather panniers, dual seat and special megaphone cans.

The author found that the Adventurer was at its best cruising along at no more than 60mph (100kph) on smooth A or B roads – or much more slowly wherever there was an audience.

The Adventurer is a polisher's dream: there is so much chrome and brightwork to keep shining. Many people go further and also have chrome chain guards and luggage racks.

There are several other machines to choose from in this retro section of the market, such as the Honda VF750C and Harley-Davidson Dyna Super Glide. In this company, Triumph's classics not only handle better but are more comfortable too, although *Bike* magazine's opinion was that machines like these are at their best when parked. A little unambitious, I would say. I think the Adventurer and Thunderbird are probably at their best cruising somewhere like the esplanade at Blackpool or Southend-on-Sea.

SPRINT

If the Adventurer was physically uncooperative above 65mph (105kph), then the Sprint was a vastly different experience. Maybe it wasn't as different as a purely sports machine, but the moment I left Ling's on the smart cherry-red number, I knew I was hooked! I found it a joy to ride, willing to be ridden fast, leaned accurately through corners, and its chassis was quite capable of handling the 900 triple's resources of power. It could also be ridden at as leisurely a pace as one liked, unlike my nutcase CBR which virtually insists on being ridden flat out all the time. With the Sprint, occasionally I even threw full-face lid and leather trousers to the

The Sprint was the most able all-rounder the author rode, partly because its riding position is set for touring, yet it still delivers a 98bhp punch when required. Maybe he was seduced by the cherry-red colour scheme, too!

winds and rode it in open-face helm. It's that kind of bike: you can go just as fast or as slow as you like, and not be burdened with the feeling that you're not doing it justice.

As you'd expect with an all-rounder, there are a number of potential competitors pitched either side of the Sprint's £8,324 price tag (1997 prices), like the Yamaha XJ900S Diversion and the BMW R110RS; and for a little more than Sprint money you could have Honda's rapid V4-engined VFR750, widely regarded as the greatest all-rounder in the business.

The Sprint is still a weighty machine: 474lb (215kg), which belies its wonderfully poised character when on the move. Several of my friends seem to live down rather long unmade gravelled tracks, which were fine to go down to show off the Tiger, but required some delicate handling on the Sprint. Turning round on gravel needs to be thought out carefully before actually stopping the bike, otherwise you can get bogged down and it will exhaust you hauling it around.

My favourite British circuits are Brands Hatch and Donington Park, and I rode the Sprint to Donington for the 1996 British Grand Prix meeting, which coincided with a round of the Speed Triple Challenge. It was a sufficiently long ride to reveal any deficiencies in the bike's make-up, but needless to say its performance was flawless. The journey there was an early morning run so I didn't meet much in the way of traffic, although about half-way there I spotted in the mirrors another bike headlight catching me up. The green and white paint scheme told me it was a Kawasaki ZXR of some kind, and although I was regularly up around 100mph (160kph), I was expecting him to come by at any time. However, he kept station fifty yards or so behind, and as we got to Leicester I had concluded that he was Donington-bound as well. Just as well, because I

At speed, the Sprint's cockpit fairing gives excellent protection against the elements and wind blasts from juggernauts.

hadn't worked out the best way of negotiating the city, and as we both stopped to fill up with petrol, he explained the best route. It turned out that his bike was a 400cc race-rep, and although extremely nimble, with only 59bhp it would have been hard-pressed to outdrag the Sprint's torquey 900, and that was why he was happy to ride with me. That's another great thing about biking: it's part of the camaraderie that on the way to an event, you link up with more and more riders going your way.

At Donington I met some of the Triumph promotions people who were giving the company's new articulated mobile shop and display vehicle its maiden outing. Predictably there were a hundred or so extremely tasty post-renaissance Triumphs there in the 'VIP' parking area around the transporter, plus a number of classics. It was swelteringly hot, and along with everybody else there, leathers were stripped off and stuffed into rucksacks, prior to doing the rounds and settling down to watch the action. Fantastic stuff it was, too!

The return journey was arduous, not so much because of traffic, but because there was a fickle cross-wind all the way across the fens to Norfolk, and high speeds were only maintained by hanging on tight and leaning into the wind. Gusts were quite alarming, and vibration levels more prominent than during the morning's ride, the more acute probably because of tiredness and the cross-wind – none of which was the bike's fault. In summary, the Sprint is two things: it's an excellent tourer, and it's also a cruise missile when you need it to be. It's probably the best all-round Triumph, unless you have a specific need to go off-road or to travel in sports mode. Personally I've had enough of that crouched riding position with the CBR – for the time being!

THE DAYTONA

The original Daytona is now perceived as the 'old' model, but at its outset it was clearly designed to be seen as the sportsbike of the Triumph range. Even now it does look the part, even if it lacks the full race-rep stance of something like a Rothmans-liveried Honda NC24, and is now shaded by the T595. The Daytona's fully faired bodywork is finished in either a bright banana-like 'racing' yellow, 'pimento' red or 'diablo' black. The dials are a sumptuous cream, highlighted by red needles and numerals, and like the other Triumphs, the controls are all logically placed. The original Daytona falls into the sports touring

category when compared with a super sports FireBlade or Exup, but it has fewer vibrations and is therefore more comfortable to ride over long distances than the big Japanese sports machines. For someone over 6ft (2m) tall, the Daytona riding position is excellent – as are all Triumphs. There is plenty of room behind the fairing, which does its job in protecting the rider from the wind at high speed. The seat is notably good on the Daytona, which is an important consideration, and the pillion also gets a reasonable ride.

The Triumph America-backed Daytona may run in the US AMA race series, but it should not be confused with purpose-built tearaways such as the Thunderace or Ninja. As sports bikes go, the Daytona is on the heavy side, tipping the scales at 466lb (210kg) dry and over 500lb (225kg) fully laden. Its centre of gravity is also relatively high, so it lacks the pin-sharp handling of, say, the 916 Ducati. Furthermore, the old Daytona's pace means that it lacks the easy-going mid-range pulling-power of its companions, while in traffic an absence of mid-range torque calls for frequent gear changes. However, it compensates with a readiness to unleash its revs, taking off at 7,000rpm and howling up to 10,000 when the rev limiter cuts in. Vibration levels seem to run at roughly the same level as the average straight four.

Actually, the motorcycle press didn't like the 1,000cc Daytona, but all comparisons are subjective to an extent, and there is no such thing as an unworthy Triumph. You have to ride them, and not take for granted what the reviewers say.

One of the attractions of BMW bikes and dispatch riders' workhorses such as the Kawasaki GT500 or the Honda NTV650 are their hassle-free shaft drives. However the Daytona's eccentric chain adjusters are of the Kawasaki type, and easy to use. Under the seat, the Daytona houses a good toolkit,

The Daytona's riding position is excellent, with plenty of room behind the full fairing, while the seat is comfortable for rider and pillion. It's a relatively heavy bike, but although its centre of gravity is quite high, it's a delight to take for a blast.

and a manual comes with it. Its front suspension is adjustable for compression and rebound damping as well as spring pre-load, unlike the original Trophy's simpler set-up, although the Daytona is easier to adjust than some sports bikes. Ground clearance is good, too.

As with the other Triumphs, the Daytona has a meaty feel about it at rest; you know you're astride a purposeful machine. It's nimble enough on the move, however, and in the fastest of sweeping turns, it responds beautifully as you lean it from side to side. If you change your line suddenly, it behaves

predictably, and somehow the higher your velocity, the better it feels. Whereas earlier models were prone to dive under hard braking, the more recent adjustable rebound damping alleviates this. So while stability is impressive, so are the brakes, and thanks to steel brake hoses and four pot calipers, stopping power is both firm yet gradual, while the Bridgestone BT50 tyres provide prodigious levels of grip. They are rather better than the Michelin M89s with which the Daytonas were originally shod, although the French rubber has a better reputation for longevity.

Despite the racing attitude of the Daytona riding position, it still has potential as a tourer – I saw a heavily laden Daytona at Gothenburg last summer, two-up as well – but as always, it is just as well to have the right machine for the job, and the 1996-spec Trophy is the quality tourer *par excellence*. And again, if it was a question of cost, you might have to settle for a secondhand Honda VFR750 or early Trophy.

THE TROPHY

Although I never rode one on a long journey, the Trophy's sculpted seat and riding position were superbly comfortable, with wide, backwards-raked bars and chunky pegs, flat rather than tubular in aspect. The screen was perhaps (unsurprisingly) more protective than the Sprint's, but optional taller ones in Lexan are available for even taller riders. However, with all its kit on board, the Trophy was undoubtedly the most cumbersome Triumph to manoeuvre when parking. Also, whereas you could get your knee down with an original 1991/1992 Trophy, the one with the best riding position and front-wheel feel, the same kind of behaviour would be quite inappropriate with a 1996 model and you'd probably come unstuck trying the same thing. Nevertheless, the Trophy 1200 I

Despite its apparent bulk, the 1996 Trophy would hold its line without wallowing.

tried handled well enough on its Bridge-stone BT54s, despite its apparent bulk – weighing in at 518lb (235kg) – and provided it was set up early for bends, it would hold its line nicely without wallowing. However, I do wonder if it might be a handful to bring to a stop if fully laden and two-up.

The big Trophy's counterbalanced four-pot 1200 is the biking equivalent of an automatic, its six-speed gearbox almost redundant, so seamless is its powerband. There can be no question of its ability to reach its projected 155mph (245kph) maximum, although you'd want to be well tucked down behind the screen to do it. As it is, 80mph (125kph) cruising is a modest 5,000rpm, with the same again until the red line. One optional extra worth considering – bearing in mind that the Trophy is already distinctly better value for money than the BMW R- and K-series – is an enclosed chain cover, which keeps it free from muck and bullets; it may not be a shaft drive, but the chain could last nearly as long.

THE NEW DAYTONA

Leaving the best – or at least the most exciting – until last, we now come to the new Daytona T595 and the T509 Speed Triple, which Ling's had as a demonstrator by March 1997. The T595 is not really like a conventional Triumph to ride, probably because the weight is carried lower down in the chassis; it is more like a cross between a Ducati 916 and a FireBlade, which is more or less what was intended. The riding position is actually more like the Japanese machine, without the cramped wrists of the Italian. But to ride, if anything it feels more akin to the Ducati than the flighty and possibly slightly faster FireBlade, although it is maybe not as delicate as the Duke. Nevertheless, its outright potential is way

ahead of my modest two-wheeling abilities, although like all Triumphs, it does inspire confidence.

As regards design, the new Daytona's state-of-the-art Nissin brakes are phenomenal, probably better than a FireBlade's; and as you might expect of a pure sports bike, there is no hint of flexing about the frame, even when throwing it with abandon round tight country bends. The steering feels beautifully balanced, neutral really, with no deviation from the chosen line. Unsurprisingly, it always feels as if there is a substantial amount of power left in reserve from the rasping triple. At 6,000rpm it takes off with a vengeance, and is still going hard at 10,000rpm. Of course there is ample available at low revs for most normal road conditions – the triple's torque was always its

Advanced riding: David Heal demonstrates supreme control on his Ongar Motorcycles-sponsored Speed Triple racer.

forte. In short, there is no doubt whatsoever that Triumph's designers and engineers got their sums absolutely right with this one – and its streetfighter sibling. The main question is, how could they do it for the money?

The motorcycling press was pretty much in agreement. This is what a few of the comics had to say about the T595 and T509, launched at the 3.5km Cartagena race circuit near Alicante in southern Spain.

Performance Bike's Jill Strong was impressed at how the T595 got its power down. 'Reams of arm-wrenching power thrust against the track through the enormous 190 rear', she enthused. The brakes were 'viciously snappy from new and needed bedding in,' while the bike 'steered beautifully' and was 'perfectly neutral ... better steering than a 916 and better stability than a CBR900.' Referring to improved ground clearance, she commented that the new Daytona 'didn't deck-out like the old, saggy sports tourers did.'

It wasn't all sweetness and light, however. *SuperBike*'s Alex Hearn reported difficulties with the ergonomics – 'my wrists were raging in pain at being trapped at such an awkward angle, and the tank was intruding where it wasn't welcome,' he complained. On the positive side, he thought the T595 'nimbler than a Thunderace ... too classy to headbang with the 'Blade ... but has brute strength that the Ducati can't match.'

The editorial team on *Fast Bikes* did a back-to-back with the T595, 916 and Fire-Blade in its February 1997 issue, and came to similar conclusions about the T595's riding position, finding the FireBlade like a 'limo', a 'sedan-chair on wheels' by comparison. But ultimately they were impressed by the Daytona's balance, '... the ZZR1100, Thunderace and co. don't come close ...' Neither had they 'ever ridden a more stable sports bike.' The T595's majestic power

delivery at 8,000rpm, they said, '... renders horizons to crinkly watery-eyed impressions.' But their unanimous verdict eventually went to the Ducati, even though the Triumph had it beaten on several counts.

Erstwhile editor of *Bike*, Phil West tested one of the first T595s in the magazine's March 1997 issue, and decided its conception was 'cold and calculated', in that it deliberately encapsulated all the desirable elements of the 916 and FireBlade. 'It's a fantastic sports bike,' he admitted, which will 'sell by the truckload, while still retaining an exclusivity bikes like the 'Blade could never manage.'

Riding the T509 was like having the cobwebs blown away – literally, as the rider's lid takes the full force of the wind on this unfaired street-fighter, as I found as I rode Ling's demonstrator. Just as with the new Suzukis, you start up the T509 with the clutch lever pulled in – disengaged in other words – and with the throttle closed. There are some excellent uncrowded roads around Watton in the East Anglian Breckland, and I was able to give the new Speed Triple its head. There was instant response to every twist of the throttle, and I felt instinctively it would go absolutely anywhere I wanted it to, it was so nicely balanced. If there was ever a faired model, I would certainly try that, and also one with the optional US-market higher bars. As *SuperBike*'s Roland Brown observed, these would give a more upright riding position – and make wheelies easier to pull! He also loved the T509's looks and praised the high spec: it gets 'the type of gear many of its unfaired rivals do without.' Of the engine, he thought 'it's closer to that of the T595 than the old lump.' And in conclusion, he said 'it delivers everything it threatens.' That is certainly clear, as the new bikes do battle on the circuits in the 1997 Speed Triple Challenge.

8 Speed Triple Challenge

Triumphs have done well in competition virtually from the marque's beginnings, notching up many successes in domestic and international races.

As a reminder of the company's heritage, it is worth mentioning one or two post-war winners: in 1946, Ernie Lyons won the Manx Grand prix on a Tiger 100, and we have Don Crossley's 1948 Senior Manx TT win on the Triumph Grand Prix road-racer. This classy machine was a limited-production bike – up to 200 units – but racing kits for the Tiger 100 were available to private entrants until 1953. The Grand Prix was considered even quicker than the Manx Nortons. And while Mike Hailwood and Don Shorey were winning the 1958 Thruxton 500 on a T110, the little Tiger Cubs were universally very successful at the other end of the competition scale, in scrambling. For a long time the T120 was recognized as the best production racer to have, and for a short time the 1965 Thruxton Bonneville was a purpose-built production racer.

However, there was no official factory competition programme until Harry Sturgeon succeeded Edward Turner in 1967. Big names from that period – the late sixties and early seventies – included John Hartle, Gary Nixon, Percy Tait, Malcolm Uphill, Paul Smart, Gene Romero, John Cooper, Tony Jefferies and Tom Dickie. Under Bert Hopwood's direction, a team of six Trident triples went into action in Europe and the States, building up a record as one of the most successful racing bikes of all time. One of the works' Tridents, 'Slippery Sam', scored five Isle of Man Production TT victories in succession from 1971 to 1975; in 1972, Ray Pickrell lifted both the Production TT and Formula 750 awards.

Motorcycle manufacturers and, to an extent, car makers, derive fabulous publicity from competition, and in many cases race-derived innovations filter through very quickly to the machines ridden on the road. Many road-going machines lend themselves to competition, such as Triumph's own Daytona and Speed Triple, but nowhere is the competition connection clearer than in a pure road-race model like the cutting-edge HRC-built Honda RC30. You can ride its 400cc race-rep version, the V4-engined NC30, for well under £4k, bought from a grey import specialist. This race-bred association fosters exceedingly powerful customer loyalty, and is an excellent marketing tool for the manufacturer.

The lesson was not lost on Triumph's Hinckley marketing people. One convenient way of establishing the reborn company in the minds of at least the committed enthusiast was to set up a factory-sponsored race series. A one-make championship would both exclude any rivals from scooping honours and publicity, and it would mean that all entrants started with a level playing field. Thus it was that in 1994, Triumph ventured into one-make production racing with the classy-looking Speed Triple. The inaugural race was held at the British

Winner of the 1996 Mobil One Speed Triple Challenge was David Jefferies, pictured astride his Allan Jefferies Motorcycles-prepared bike on the Triumph stand at the 1996 NEC Show.

Grand Prix meeting at Donington, and the format was so popular that entrants were drawn from Australia and South America, with races staged in the States, France and Germany. This was a one-off race, providing the launch pad for the series proper which would start in 1995.

Regulations were drawn up in conjunction with the Motorcycle Circuit Racing Control Board to FIM international status. Grids of up to forty machines were anticipated, and the entry fee was £70 per race with a registration fee of £120; this was good value

compared with competition entry fees generally. Each competitor is allocated a race number which he keeps for the whole season. In 1996 the Speed Triple Challenge consisted of eight rounds, usually of ten laps' duration, held at some of the UK's most interesting and demanding circuits: Mallory Park, Cadwell Park, Donington Park, Brands Hatch, Oulton Park and Silverstone. These ranged from the Transatlantic meeting and the British Motorcycle Grand Prix, both held at Donington, to the International Trophy at Silverstone.

Points were allocated on a scale of twenty-five for a win, twenty for second and sixteen for third, down to one point for fifteenth place. The company and its sponsors provided a total budget of £75,000, with prize fund of £7,940 for each round, ranging from £2k plus a trophy for the winner, down to £150 for fifteenth place. Race organizers' sponsorship also paid out lap money on the basis of £25 for completing each of the first three laps, £15 for the middle distance laps, and £50 for the last three laps. The icing on the cake was the championship winner's award of a new 1996 production Speed Triple bike. A further reward was the presentation of the Squib Burton Trophy – a silver cup – at three Donington rounds, taken by the top points-scoring British rider. Squib Brown was a dirt-track rider who won the first-ever race at Donington in 1931 on a 348cc Raleigh, and he donated his trophy to be used as an annual award for solo motorcycles. The roll of honour for this prize includes Ron Haslam, Steve Hislop and Terry Rymer.

As at all competition events, bikes and riders' gear are subjected to official scrutiny both before and, in the case of the leading machines, after each race, and can be rejected on the grounds of safety or failure to comply with the regulations. The series' technical officer has the jurisdiction to have bikes stripped for inspection, although in practice this is rare. Bikes are held in *parc ferme* after the race. There is a fifteen-minute practice session before each race, with best lap times counting for grid positions; entrants have to complete three laps of practice to qualify. The grids are in four-four-four formation.

STANDARD ISSUE

In order to maintain a high standard of presentation, and to preserve the Speed Triple identity, all original panels, cowling and mudguards have to be retained. The Triumph logo and that of the principal sponsor Mobil have to be clearly visible, although the bike can be painted or liveried to whatever the rider's personal sponsorship dictates. The chassis frame has to remain standard, as must the saddle and seat hump. Petrol tanks should also be unmodified, and contain a minimum of two litres of fuel at the end of a race. All extraneous functions can be removed. Rear footrests and hangers can go, as should side and centre stands, front headlight, mirrors horn and indicators. Minimum dry weight limit is 485lb (220kg), which is actually greater that the old Speed Triple's 460lb (209kg) in standard road-going trim. Despite being stripped of all unnecessary kit, the Speed Triple still manages to look more or less the sort of bike that you or I can ride on the road, and in this respect it is easy to identify with the competitors on the track.

The regulations stipulate original wheels, shod with any of the big names' racing tyres: Avon, Dunlop, Bridgestone, Pirelli, Metzeler or Michelin all produce suitable race rubber. Tyre warmers are used while on the grid, removed a minute before the start. While the speedo can be removed, the tacho has to be the Triumph original. Alternators have to be standard, rev limiters cannot be removed, although braided brake hoses are fine and choice of brake pads is free. Original air-boxes must be retained, while carbs, apart from the main jet, must also be unmodified. There is free choice of Triumph's standard rear sprockets, and chains must be 9.65mm standard issue.

Only standard Speed Triple engines qualify, and nothing may exceed 100bhp; anything over this is excluded. To provide better ground clearance, competitors can fit the company's own competition exhaust system. Standard five- or six-speed gearboxes

While lean and trim, the Speed Triple Challenge bikes don't require too many alterations to comply with race regulations; modifications include fitting an oil cooler and steering damper, while lights and stands are removed for lightness. This bike was ridden during the 1996 season by Paul Brown.

have to be fitted, and upgrading from five to six gears is allowed. In deference to the series' main sponsor, all bikes must use Mobil 1 Racing 40 oil, with no additives.

Stiffer springs and valving can be incorporated in the front suspension provided the original outer covers are used. The rear suspension linkage has to be standard, but the actual unit can be swapped for Triumph's uprated version.

THRILLS AND SPILLS

Motorcycle racing is in general far more spectacular than car racing. For a start you can actually see, and up to a point identify with what the riders are doing. It never fails to thrill, and one can only marvel at the sheer courage and skill of riders who pull off amazing stunts lap after lap, and even after high-siding into the scenery think nothing of getting back on and doing it all over again. The Speed Triple Challenge is no exception. Because they are production machines, they are relatively slower than the superbikes, and are, if anything, as popular with the riders for that reason. Racing them presents a slightly different sort of challenge.

The Jack Lilley Motorcycles Speed Triple was raced by Peter Graves and Mark Linscott during 1996.

Possibly no single event encapsulated the 1996 Speed Triple season more than the final round at Donington, when series leader David Jefferies consolidated his position at the top of the table, finishing tenth, despite being in agony from an accident at Schwantz curve during Superbike practice. He had to finish higher than fourteenth to clinch the title. The race was won by Mike Edwards from Michael Rutter and Alan Batson. David Jefferies' closest challenger in the quest for the title was Paul Brown, who needed to win the race to overtake Jefferies' twenty-four point advantage. Largely due to front-end problems, he only managed fourth, however, beating the outgoing Speed Triple champion of 1995, Mark Phillips in the process.

It was by no means a straightforward affair. Fighting back after a poor start had left him in fourth place off the grid, Mike Edwards managed to overhaul Michael Rutter on the leading machine, passing him when the latter's bike slid; but it was a close-run thing to the chequered flag. Meanwhile, Jefferies' pit crew was keeping him posted about arch-rival Brown's position on every lap, and as it turned out he had done enough to clinch the crown. Final championship standings were David Jefferies on 125 points, Paul Brown with 108 and Alan Batson on 101, followed by Ray Stringer (81), David Heal (74) and Michael Rutter (71). Mike Edwards finished eighth with 61 points, while other race winners in the series were Mick Corrigan (62) and Alan Lewis (48).

By 1997, the Speed Triple Challenge was finished. The Daytona 600 was the machine to take over the company's sporting mantle when, in 2003, Triumph ValMoto scorched to a stunning and historic victory in the Isle of Man Junior TT. The British manufacturer had not won on the island for twenty-eight years, however, 34-year-old Bruce Anstey

and his Triumph ValMoto Daytona 600 proved to be the day's dominant force around the legendary Mountain Course. Anstey finished 10.96 seconds ahead of his nearest rival and recorded the fastest ever Supersport TT race, which he completed in 1:15.13.98. A trio of Triumph ValMoto Daytona 600s took on the Japanese machinery and all three finished. The team's two other riders, Jim Moodie and John McGuinness, took 9th and 10th.

Founded in 2002 by Jack Valentine's V&M racing team, ValMoto formed a partnership with Triumph to campaign a two-rider team in the British Supersport Championship. Following a promising debut season in the domestic series, the team continued its campaign in 2004 with just one rider – Craig Jones. The teenager won his first race at the final round of the season. Apart from the TT success, Triumph ValMoto also claimed victory at Macau as well as three other top three finishes in leading public road races.

Although Triumph withdrew from racing at the end of the year, the company returned to the American road racing scene in 2005 with the Thruxton Cup Challenge, billed as part of the AHRMA (American Historic Racing Motorcycles Association) national schedule. The machines resemble stock bikes available ex showroom. The series was limited to the Thruxton 900, the café racer model with its clip-on handle-bars, seat hump and 865cc twin-cylinder engine, the most powerful of Triumph's twin-cylinder line-up. The first season of competition saw motorcycle legends Gary Nixon and Jay Springsteen joining the fray along with assorted celebrities, journalists, Triumph dealers, new riders, and experienced road racers. The Thruxton Cup Challenge was set to return for 2006 with grids just as big as the first season and promising some of the most exciting battles on American soil.

9 Transformation Complete

It's amazing how time flies. And amazing how much Triumph has evolved during the past decade. When The Crowood Press asked me to update this book I called Bruno Tagliaferri to see what there was in the way of fresh material, and he explained that even the management structure had shifted as the company had grown. He was still head of sales and marketing, but PR had become a separate function, with an outside agency also involved in the dissemination of information. The changes were indicative of a company full of confidence and forging off to embrace pastures new.

The main landmarks in the firm's history during this interim period stand out clearly. Most significant of these was the opening of the new plant. T2, as it is known, lies in Normandy Way at the outer reaches of the Dodwell's Bridge Road industrial estate, almost within shouting distance of the 'old' T1 factory in Jacknell Road on which the first edition of this book was based. The main point about the new T2 plant – hardly new anymore, but for the moment 'new' serves to distinguish it from T1 – is that the manufacturing process is the same as before, with few exceptions and innovations. It's just all on a much grander scale than T1.

In March 2002, a fire destroyed the old T1 assembly and dispatch areas. Luckily, everything at T2 was already in place and most systems were functioning, which partly explains why the blaze didn't cause too much of an interruption in the production process. And that brings us to the new models, none more clearly encapsulating the company's

After the disastrous fire of 2002, production was transferred to the new, much larger T2 plant, not far away in Normandy Way on the fringe of Hinckley's Dodwell's Bridge Road industrial estate.

The Thunderbird continued to be the mainstay of the classic cruiser brigade into the 21st century, but by 2003 it had effectively been superseded by the Speedmaster and America versions of the Bonneville. A sportier version of the retro-styled Thunderbird was the Sport, with a three-into-one upswept pipe and pancake air filter.

brave, almost maverick attitude than the magnificent Rocket III.

Judging Triumph against the standards it set itself when it relaunched in 1990, the company has surpassed all expectations. To stand a chance of survival it had to be different and it had to take chances. But it did its sums carefully and, as we saw in the 1990s, it took a succession of carefully considered steps forward, keeping up with, and in some cases staying ahead of, the leading manufacturers and their talismans. That way it developed a set of machines that catered for every niche of biking, with varying specifications honed to pander to the most finicky of tastes.

As we have seen, Triumph consolidated its niche in the nostalgia market in the mid-1990s with the Thunderbird and its Americanesque Adventurer sibling. That meant it was well placed, five years on, to introduce the 790cc and 865cc versions of the iconic Bonneville, T100 and Thruxton Bonneville, based on classic 2-cylinder engine technologies and frame design. These three models were convincing iterations of their 1950s and 1960s predecessors, not merely because of the new parallel-twin engine but because the styling and *ambiance* were just right as well.

By 2006, the classic range encompassed the Bonneville, T100 and fabulous Bonneville Scrambler, plus the dramatic Thruxton 900. In the equally evocative cruiser line-up were

It had to come eventually and, sure enough, in September 2000 Triumph revived the revered Bonneville name along with a new parallel-twin to power it. Both pistons of the 790cc twin rose and fell together via a 360-degree crankshaft firing interval, calculated to produce the distinctive feel of a classic British twin – but without the oil leaks. It developed 90 per cent of its peak 60Nm of torque at 3,500rpm, which it sustained all the way to the red line via its five-speed gearbox. The T100 version was equipped with the 865cc (90 × 68mm) version of the parallel twin.

The 2003 Daytona 955i could do 168mph (270kph) and was a fantastic machine for track days, where its beautifully balanced chassis worked to best effect. The aluminium frame was allied to a single-sided swing-arm, fully adjustable 45mm telescopic forks and a rear monoshock. Tyre sizes were 120/70 ZR17 front and 190/50 ZR17 rear, slowed by twin four-piston calipers up front acting on 320mm floating discs, and a single twin-piston caliper working on the 220mm rear disc.

Retro design is big business, and Triumph has plenty of classic icons to exploit. High on the list of reiterations of earlier models was the 865cc 70bhp Thruxton Bonneville, with high-lift cams, which recalled the marque's halcyon days as a competition machine as well as its heyday as a café racer. Key features were the clip-ons, seat hump and short competition front mudguard.

(Left) *In 2000, the TT600 took Triumph into the hothouse world of 4-cylinder sports bikes and the frenetic 600 supersport category. The 599cc DOHC in-line four developed 89bhp and could hit 145mph (233kph), and had excellent handling and brakes. Its successor in 2003 was the Daytona 600 four, which won the Isle of Man TT in that year. The TT600 frame and mechanicals also provided the basis for the street-fighter Speed Four.*

(Right) *While it was an excellent machine in its own right, the TT600 didn't quite hit the spot as far as the mass market was concerned owing to its bland styling (by Japanese standards perhaps) and a reputation for poor fuel injection and throttle response in the mid-range sector. It thus became something of a bargain in the second-hand market, and main dealers subsequently carried the fuel-injection remap programme to sort out performance issues.*

the America and the Speedmaster, and, of course, the 2.2-litre Rocket III, quite the most outrageous concept of, well, of all time really, taking the triple to extremes.

In the competitive sweatbox of the sports bike world, Triumph was quite capable of going head to head with Japanese manufacturers. The flagship Daytona 955i was regularly compared with the CBR900 Fire Blade and Ducati 916, and the Hinckley product frequently came out on top, although it was eventually outgunned by the newer Yamaha R1 and GSX-R1000. In the late 1990s and early years of the new millennium, no segment was as fiercely competitive as the 600cc sports bike category. The new TT and 4-cylinder Daytona 600 held their own against the

Japanese makers, although by 2005 the TT600 had been superseded by the Daytona 650. This was a stroked version of the 600cc model, using the same liquid-cooled, fuel-injected, DOHC, 16-valve, in-line 4-cylinder motor, but with a longer stroke (increased by 3.1mm to 44.5mm) and with capacity boosted by 47cc to 646cc. It was a deliberate ploy to distance the Triumph product from the maelstrom of Japanese 600s, and it won the day with top-end power bolstered with gobbets of mid-range torque.

The T509 street-fighter morphed into the 955i Speed Triple, which was irresistible as far as I was concerned; I became smitten with the lipstick-pink hue known by the factory as nuclear red. I found one at Rettendon

The beam-frame Daytona 675 triple of 2006 took over from the TT600 in the mad sports bike arena, its extra capacity placing it on another plane from the majority of 600 fours. The spars of the fabricated, open-back, cast-aluminium frame wrapped over the top of the motor, with the exhaust emerging under the seat. The rake was set at an angle of 23.5 degrees and the trail at 86.8mm within a 1,392mm wheelbase. The Kayaba 41mm upside-down forks were fully adjustable for spring preload, rebound and compression damping, as was the Kayaba piggyback reservoir rear damper. The aluminium swing-arm was a two-piece casting measuring 574mm from rear-wheel spindle to pivot point, while the dry weight was 363lb (165kg). The brand-new 675cc motor was extremely compact and narrow, a water-cooled, 3-cylinder, 12-valve unit that contributed to the bike's overall slimness. Induction was by a Keihin closed-loop fuel-injection system involving a trio of 44mm throttle bodies and three twelve-point multi-spray injectors. The stacked six-speed gearbox shortened the engine considerably, and the model was the first Triumph to feature a truly close ratio set-up for all six speeds. Bore and stroke was 74.0 × 52.3mm, with 125bhp maximum power delivered at a zinging 12,500rpm, and 72Nm of torque at 11,750rpm.

in Essex that belonged to a collector and had blue after-market radiator cladding and belly-pan – it had only done about 800 miles (1,300km) and it was love at first sight. Subsequently I installed a pillion grab rail that matched the aluminium of the chassis frame, and when it was recalled to Lings for a new fuel line I got them to fit heated grips; the benefit in winter was marginal, as only the first two fingers on each hand registered any warmth. Then I had the saddle repadded, largely at the request of my boy Alfie – our lengthy 40-mile (60km) school run from Norwich to Leiston was just a touch too far for his 13-year-old backside without a comfort stop.

In 2005 the Speed Triple received a facelift, and in its 1.05-litre guise it looked

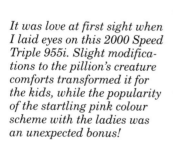

It was love at first sight when I laid eyes on this 2000 Speed Triple 955i. Slight modifications to the pillion's creature comforts transformed it for the kids, while the popularity of the startling pink colour scheme with the ladies was an unexpected bonus!

In its 2002 incarnation the Sprint ST was a match for the benchmark VFR800. As well as being a more characterful bike – largely thanks to its 955i triple power plant – it was also as much at home scratching as touring.

even more radical, what with its high-rise exhaust system. Along with its sibling, the 600 Speed Four from 2003, the Speed Triple ruled the street-fighter category, if not in outright performance then certainly in perception and image. In the interests of a stubby superstructure, the pillion was even more minimal than its predecessor's, forging a bonding experience between rider and passenger at the expense of creature comfort, while the rear number plate was superfluous to the design. On a work trip to Zagreb in 2005, I noted the fashion among bikers for mounting the plate at an acute angle so that it tucked back under the saddle; an aesthetic improvement, certainly, but one that was unlikely to find favour with PC Plod.

The Sprint ST was often rated by our esteemed bike press as being as 'together' as a VFR800 but not as boring, which, having owned one of Honda's cooking sport tourers for a while, is a sentiment I can vouch for. However, the only reason I would have wanted a Sprint more than a Speed Triple was that, being clad in plastic, it would have been easier to keep clean. Personally I like the sit-up riding position of the Speed Triple, as opposed to the dropped-wrists

attitude of the Sprint ST. In 1999, the RS version of the Sprint was launched, a more sports-oriented machine than the fully faired ST – only the top half was faired and the sports handlebars were set lower. The RS lasted until 2004, but never really

Sports riders who wanted something slightly less focused than the Daytona, yet more engrossing than the Sprint ST, could opt for the Sprint RS with its half-fairing and lower-set grips. Seen as a budget sports tourer, the 108bhp RS was in production between 2000 and 2004.

gripped the imagination; if you wanted a sports bike you went for a Daytona or maybe a TT.

While the 955i Daytona and Speed Triple had an aluminium-tube frame, the Sprints were beam-framed. This was a logical progression from the spine frame of the early 1990s models, giving high degrees of rigidity and, hence, handling. The 110bhp engine was finished in black and exposed as a styling point. A conventional swing-arm that replaced the ST's single-sider cut out unsprung weight, thereby making the rear damper (which was 5mm longer) more responsive, albeit at the expense of a redesigned exhaust system to achieve better ground clearance.

The original Tiger was one of my favourite models when I first researched this book, and I loved the semi-abstract graphics. The facelifted bike doesn't have the same 'don't mess with me' stance, and looks more spindly, with inferior graphics

to my mind. In 2001, the Tiger received the 955cc triple engine in 104bhp format, plus a new exhaust, gearbox, injection system and reworked engine internals. Colour-coded factory panniers repositioned the Tiger as more of a grand tourer, although you could have done that to the original model. Whether it would stand up to the sort of punishment meted out on something like the Ewan McGregor/Charley Boorman *Long Way Round* adventure is another matter (although I'd be happy to give it a go if Triumph would like to sponsor me!).

In 2002 the suspension internals were revised to make the ride much firmer and more suited to roads. Two years later there was a major make-over that included cast-alloy wheels instead of wire spokes, a different swing-arm and panniers, heated grips and a centre stand as standard. The 2006 Tiger came with rerouted coolant hoses and wiring, while in terms of mechanics it featured an improved gear change and

Running the same 1050cc 3-cylinder unit as the Speed Triple, the 2005 Sprint ST was a logical evolution of the refined sports tourer, built on an aluminium beam frame with a 1,454mm wheelbase. Peak power was 125bhp at 9,250rpm, with a maximum torque of 104Nm arriving at 5,000rpm. The 43mm cartridge telescopic front forks were adjustable for spring preload, while the rear shock was remotely adjustable for spring preload and rebound damping. The Sprint ST featured Triumph's ABS, operating at 100 calculations per second, and acting via a pair of four-pot brake calipers mated to 320mm floating discs at the front and a two-pot caliper and single 255mm disc at the back. In 2006, this was the best Triumph to

transmission backlash eliminator, plus the 1050cc engine cases used in the all-new Speed Triple and Sprint ST, although it still had an engine capacity of only 955cc. The appearance has since been beefed up with the fitting of alloy spoke wheels, while optional matching panniers emphasize the bike's role as a tourer, albeit one that'll make it down a forest track, if not a peat bog.

BLAZING SADDLES

Now we shall regress for a moment. As Triumph's bike range rolled into the new millennium, plans for the T2 plant came to

The original Hinckley Tiger was given a major make-over in 2001, when it was transformed into a more rangy looking bike, running with a tuned-down version of the 955i engine. The steering and frame geometry had the rake set at an angle of 25.8 degrees and the trail at 92mm, with a wheelbase of 1,515mm. The compliant front forks employed single-rate springs while the rear shock's spring preload could be remotely adjusted. The new fuel-tank capacity was 5.3gal (24 litres), providing a useful range for regular touring.

fruition, and by 2001 construction was underway. But then came the fire. On the evening of Friday, 15 March 2002, an inferno destroyed two-thirds of the factory. The enormity of the conflagration can be gauged by the numbers of firemen present: more than 120 from three counties were called to tackle the blaze. One was hospitalized with minor injuries, but he seems to have been the only casualty; none of the 650-strong workforce was involved, and many senior Triumph personnel were away at Cartagena for the launch of the Daytona 600. It took more than five hours to bring the flames under control, with firemen pumping water from a nearby canal, and the site was not pronounced safe until as many days later.

The building worst affected contained the firm's original assembly line, as well as facilities for manufacturing and assembling the engines. This was also where completed bikes were checked for quality. A day's worth of production amounting to around a hundred bikes was destroyed. The principal damage occurred in the assembly area, bringing production to a standstill. Fortunately, there was a relatively large volume of undistributed stock in hand – as many as 1,800 bikes – which had been produced in advance to meet the anticipated increased demand of the coming spring, and to fulfil orders for two-and-a-half months ahead. The two machines in short supply as a result of the fire were the chromed-up Bonneville T100 Centennial Special and the new Speed Four street-fighter. All the T100s constructed had deposits paid on them. Triumph's insurance company faced a bill of more than £25 million to rebuild the factory, a pay-out that also covered workers' wages and lost income from sales.

The most likely cause of the fire was petrol fumes from fuelled-up bikes coming off the end of the assembly line prior to testing. It is thought that these fumes were ignited by the exposed pilot light of a central-heating boiler.

To expand on that hypothesis, you'll recall from earlier on in the book that once bikes reach the end of the assembly line they're fuelled up and then tested on the dyno, after which the petrol is drained off. Here's where it gets scary. The whole assembly area was engulfed in flames, and if anyone had been in there at the time, they'd have been toast. The immolation was so spontaneous that there wasn't even time for the automatic fire doors to close. Just outside the assembly area, the flames ripped through the stores and thence took hold in some recently built workshops at the rear of the plant. Incredibly, the nearby paint shop with its highly inflammable fluids

escaped; if those had gone up, the devastation would have been much worse. Though drained of fuel, the tanks of the bikes in the dispatch area were still full of vapour, and as the fire overtook them they exploded like grenades. By this time, alarms were going off and maintenance staff working at the far end of the factory had alerted the fire brigade.

Out of the ashes, the Triumph production line rose again – just up the road at the T2 plant in Normandy Way, where the firm had already been transferring production over the previous two years. The Bonneville's 2-cylinder engine was already in production at T2, as were the robotics for making chassis

Triumph has always been expert on detailing, as exemplified by the dial (in kph), bar mounts and tank-mounted rev-counter on this Speedmaster, paying obvious homage to the Milwaukee clan.

The hefty raked-out forks, pegs, bars and saddle indicated exactly where the 2003 Speedmaster street-rod 865cc twin was targeted: straight at the Harley-Davidson market. There was one fundamental difference, however: the Triumph product came with vibration-free power from its 55bhp twin thanks to its 270-degree crank firing interval.

Another take on Triumph's illustrious past was the Bonneville-based Scrambler, a direct reference to the Trophy Trail of three decades earlier. The specification was totally modern, however: the 865cc, DOHC, 8-valve, air-cooled engine operated with a 270-degree crank firing interval. With wire-spoked wheels, high-rise pipes and a decent saddle, it looked the part and was a thoroughly appealing leisure machine.

and swing-arms, while many of the bikes for distribution were in store there. There was even a sense of relief that the new assembly area would now be larger than the cramped confines of T1, and that R & D staff could take advantage of the hiatus caused by the fire to hone new machines such as the Rocket III and updated TT600.

Unfazed, Triumph also insisted that the marque's centenary celebrations should continue as planned on 15 June at Towcester racecourse, Northamptonshire. Riders were invited to bring their oldest bikes along, and like the Queen's Golden Jubilee celebrations,

the evening culminated with a major fireworks display and a laser show that flagged up historical milestones. In the USA, groups of riders took part in the epic 'Triumph Across America' run to mark the occasion. Starting in North Hampton, New Hampshire, the rally lasted two weeks and covered 4,200 miles (6,750km), visiting fourteen dealers along the way. At times there were more than 200 Triumphs travelling in formation across the States. The climax was a huge gala party for 2,000-plus guests on Colorado Boulevard, Pasadena, opposite the legendary Johnson Motors.

New for 2004, the Rocket III featured the biggest purpose-built motorcycle engine ever, at 2294cc, and could top 150mph (240kph). The chassis consisted of a large tubular steel twin-spine frame housing the big triple, while a maintenance-free shaft-drive relayed power to the supercar-sized 240/50-section rear tyre.

Just a hundred days after the inferno at T1, Triumph was in a buoyant mood. Pictures were released of the Bonneville Scrambler, a modern take on the 1960s Trophy Trail, and the Daytona 600 was released at the NEC in November 2002. Key features of the new machine included a lighter, reworked version of the TT600 motor with power boosted to 110bhp, a completely redesigned fuel-injection system, a lighter, shorter chassis, redesigned suspension and smaller, lighter brakes, all clad in radically styled fairings.

Now Triumph entered the world of the muscle cruiser. Announced on 22 August 2003, the Rocket III possessed twice as much torque as an R1, could top 150mph (240kph) and, at 2294cc, had the biggest purpose-built motorcycle engine ever. The 3-cylinder cruiser harnessed 140bhp, delivering almost twice as much torque as a Harley-Davidson V-Rod and fully 50 per cent more than a Suzuki Hayabusa. Peak torque arrived at a low 2,500rpm, and the resulting acceleration was equivalent to 1.2g; by comparison, a Suzuki GSX-R struggled to better 1g.

When researching a story for *911 & Porsche World* magazine on the V-Rod, whose water-cooled V-twin engine was designed by Porsche, I rode a Rocket III as a back-to-back comparison with the Harley. At a whisker under £12,000, the Rocket had the advantage of being a full £2,000 cheaper than the Harley. It did not disappoint. On opening the throttle, the 700lb (320kg) leviathan lunged forwards with huge force – even though I was expecting monster muscle, it did come as a bit of a shock, perhaps something to do with the enormity of scale of the whole package. I felt a bit like a human cannonball in a circus. And, of course, if it's attention you're seeking, the Rocket III has no peers. People loved it. Van drivers rubber-necked, young women waved, other riders on similarly large machines nodded, and I was treated like Mr Cool down the biker pub.

The factory figures claim the Rocket III is quicker to the ton than an R1, and its 0–60mph (0–97kph) time of 2.8 seconds is just awesome. All the action happens pretty much below 4,000rpm, which is the equivalent of 110mph (177kph). That's the same sort of territory as the V-Rod, which I didn't much care to take above 85–90mph (135–145kph) because of its feet-forward ride – quite odd on a bendy road until you get used to it. Wind

The 3-cylinder Rocket III developed 140bhp and could produce nearly twice the torque of a Harley-Davidson V-Rod, peaking at a low 2,500rpm and with a resulting 1.2g of acceleration force. The front brakes were sports-bike spec twin four-piston calipers with 320mm floating discs, while the rear brake was a twin-piston Brembo caliper acting on a 316mm disc. The 43mm upside-down forks and twin rear shocks were also specially built.

buffeting is similar, and the Rocket III with moth screen option would be my choice. Despite its size, or perhaps because of it, the bike was susceptible to buffeting from cross-winds, although given clement weather the Rocket is a relaxing ride.

Handling on the Rocket III is very good, considering its bulk and character. Ride quality is excellent, although the suspension is on the bouncy side of soft. It feels stable, with neutral steering, but with a tendency to understeer on corners where you need to show due respect. Is this a straight-road bike, then? It is certainly just right for the American market, where it can lope along all day. There is enough power – in spades – to rush past sluggardly traffic; it's a long-road bike, and it doesn't matter if the road's dual carriageway or not. The Rocket rider cruises nonchalantly at somewhere around the legal maximum, and only a trail of diesel on a corner presents any real hazard to a machine that is uncomfortable going fast on winding roads. But give it a long, straight stretch as far as the eye can see, and the Rocket laps it up. It's about easy riding – the perfect cruiser.

THAI CHEAP

At the time of the T1 fire, Triumph had also recently built a new factory near Bangkok in Thailand, and in the aftermath of the blaze there were concerns that it would follow the lead of vacuum-cleaner-maker Dyson in relocating production abroad. However, Triumph maintained that the Thai plant would concentrate on making components such as cans, which up until then had been bought in.

By 2004, the Thai facility was involved in making frames and swing-arms for certain models. As at Hinckley, the manufacturing processes included tube-cutting, bending, machining, MIG welding, EDP plating and

powder coating. Some sports bike frames were divided into a front and rear. The swing-arms produced in Thailand were the twin-sided aluminium-alloy type; the Tiger from the 2003 model year was the last to use a twin-sided swing-arm with eccentric chain adjuster. Most header components were stainless steel. The cut and bent parts were fabricated by MIG welding, while finishes varied from plain metal to electro-polishing and chrome plating for the classic bikes. Fuel tanks, oil tanks, mudguards and various chrome-plated covers were also fabricated in Thailand, using laser trimming and polishing.

TOUR GUIDE

In June 2004, factory tours started up again at T2, which is something all bikers and Triumph fans in particular should do. Basically you walk around the factory with an audio headset guide, taking in the production and assembly lines on the way. It's a treat to gaze at the bikes under construction and see the apparent ease with which the operators perform their tasks. They make it all look so simple – even ballet-like sometimes. The tours take place nine times a week, with twenty visitors on each one. Places can be booked through the firm's official dealers, of which there are fifty-five in the UK. (By comparison, there are 174 Triumph outlets in the USA, and you can access dealerships worldwide via the company' website, www.triumph.co.uk.)

I didn't get around to making the pilgrimage to the new plant until 2004, when the new Rocket III, Sprint and Speed Triple were starting to go down the line. It was a memorable trip for more than one reason. Riding my Speed Triple 955i from Norfolk to Hinckley, my journey was in the company of no less than fourteen traffic policemen, all astride their own personal bikes of one sort or another, ranging from a CBR1100 Blackbird to a Moto Guzzi. Several were aboard Triumphs. As we headed along the A14 dual carriageway via Newmarket and north of Cambridge to Kettering, they commanded the fast lane, riding in echelon; absolutely nothing came past us. More to the point, I have never felt more secure travelling fast than I did that day. When we reached the M6 they just took off; I followed into three figures and still there was no sign of the guys ahead. Soon enough I spotted an exodus onto the A5 – instead of the M69 I'd been expecting to use – and thence onto the spasmodic dual carriageway up to Hinckley. Prior knowledge meant I found the factory sooner than some, but it was an extremely good-humoured party once we got there.

After the factory tour there was a Q & A session over coffee, and someone asked what had happened to the project that was meant to be building the first 200mph (320kph) production bike. It seemed that, from 2001, the factory had been developing a 1300cc 180bhp supersport bike to rival the Hayabusa and Kawasaki ZX-12R, reputedly

at a cost of £4 million. Triumph's intention was that it should be the first production machine to break the 200mph (320kph) barrier, and the rumour was that it would be called the Daytona 1300 or Hurricane 1300. But we learnt that it had been dropped because the company felt the supersport market had peaked, so the bike wouldn't be profitable and would only ever be perceived as a curiosity. Of the seven prototypes, just one survives in the company's private museum. Well, the world needs icons – after all, what's the Rocket III if it's not an icon?

Clearly, the company is putting out an impressive roster of machines, catering for virtually every strand of the motorcycling faith. Where do I perceive a gap? Well, there's no proper scrambler, and no out-and-out motocrosser or KTM equivalent that you'd choose for the Paris–Dakar. Also, the big Trophy tourer concept is well overdue for a rethink, as the Tiger is obviously not a dedicated touring bike. As I write this update in spring 2006, the company is evidently in fine shape to conceive and build fine bikes; in fact, it has proved that it can make anything it feels like or, more aptly, anything the market

The Speed Triple was the stripped-for-action muscle bike of the Triumph range, retaining the bug-eye headlights and tube frame from the days of the T509, but given more attitude with a high-rise exhaust system. In its 1050cc triple incarnation in 2006, peak power was lifted to 130bhp @ 9,100rpm, while its peak torque of 105Nm came in at a relatively low 5,100rpm. The fully adjustable 43mm upside-down forks and rear monoshock were specifically developed for the bike.

(Above) *The Daytona 955i was still revered as an outstanding sports bike by 2006, one that could match an R1 but with styling cues that distinguished it from its Japanese counterparts. Now considered long in the tooth, it had a fuel-injected 955cc 3-cylinder engine that developed 147bhp with a peak torque of 100Nm arriving at 8,200rpm.*

(Right) *By 2005 the 955cc Tiger enduro had received alloy spoked wheels and was perceived more as a serious touring bike than a big trailie, even though it was still an able machine when the blacktop ran out. Mechanical revisions for 2006 included a slicker shift, a new cylinder head and crankcases, and a neater engine exterior, with power rated at 105bhp and 92Nm of torque.*

will buy. With annual capacity running at around 50,000 machines, Triumph has transformed itself from a niche player into a serious motorcycle manufacturer competing on the world stage with the best of them.

Just as the new factory was coming on stream, the company subjected itself to a huge internal review between 2002 and 2004. This was underpinned by the most comprehensive consumer research Triumph had ever undertaken, focusing on marketing aspects such as its brand image and corporate identity as well as global communications. Commercial director Tue Mantoni explained: 'We've comprehensively reviewed Triumph's strategy. All aspects of the business, from brand to product to dealers, were examined to help us reach our current position. Our

The days of the long-lived big Trophy tourer were at an end by 2003. Seemingly monstrous when stationary, with a huge fairing and screen up front, the Trophy was a magnificent open-road mile-muncher when it was up and running.

Triples going down the line at the T2 factory. Although the new plant was much more spacious than the first Hinckley plant in Jacknell Road, the methodology and working practices were much the same.

Another take on the custom cruiser theme was the Bonneville America, which, like the Speedmaster, sought to capitalize on Stateside easy-riding styles and the cult of 1970s Japanese customs, coupled with the evocative Triumph nomenclature and a 790cc 2-cylinder engine. It had a 270-degree firing interval – rather than the Bonneville's 360-degree – which emitted a different exhaust note and gave the bike an alternative character.

global retail sales increased by more than 25 per cent last year and we're on an aggressive drive to continue this level of growth to 2008.'

Following the review, the consensus was that Triumph should focus on its traditional strengths of character and heritage. The aim would be to draw in existing owners and attract potential new customers by exploiting the passion and charisma of Triumph bikes, as well as the inherent sex appeal of the motorcycle scene. More specifically, the company wanted its image to be evocative of top-rank Hollywood icons such as Marlon Brando, Steve McQueen, James Dean, Richard Gere and Tom Cruise, all of whom have ridden Triumphs on the silver screen.

An example of the way Triumph set out to surf that particular wave was its link-up with fashion designer Paul Smith. Not only were items of Triumph-branded biker gear styled and stocked by Paul Smith and his outlets, but he lent his hand to customized paint jobs for bikes as well. As part of the launch of the 'Triumph by Paul Smith' autumn/winter 2005 clothing and accessory

Fashion designer Paul Smith came up with some pop-art designs for the Bonneville T100 to add a touch of 1960s flavour. A hundred machines were customized in two different styles for sale on a first-come first-served basis over the winter of 2004/5.

Mean 'n' moody, the 1050cc Speed Triple in its 2005 street-fighter guise was even more macho than its previous incarnation and proved immensely popular in southern Europe. Its LED rear-light unit and clear-lens indicators complemented the bike's trademark twin bug-eye headlights. The Speed Triple's junior sibling, the 599cc 16-valve 4-cylinder naked Speed Four, was equally at home striking a pose, but lacked the aggressive rasp of the bigger triple.

collection, the designer customized nine Bonneville T100s with one-off paint schemes. Some people have all the fun jobs! These particular machines weren't actually for sale but were used as promotional items. However, the public response was so positive that Triumph elected to produce two limited-edition Paul Smith designs for sale, the so-called Multi-Union and Live Fast models, which feature special hand-painted bodywork and mock-croc leather seats. Fifty of each were up for grabs, all individually numbered and authenticated with a certificate signed by Paul Smith and John Bloor. So are these collectors' items to be incarcerated for the duration, or bikes to be ridden down the pub? You choose: they cost £7,800 on the road from any Triumph dealership, on a first-come, first-served basis, which seemed to me like a bargain – a special edition for not much more than Speed Triple money. Then again, I know which one I'd have and it wouldn't be the oldie!

Specialist motor manufacturers such as Lotus, Morgan and Caterham tend to foster owners' clubs and race series, and some, like TVR, have fiercely loyal adherents. Triumph Motorcycles looks after its customers through RAT (Riders' Association of Triumph), which has expanded in the last

decade to run many more diverse events and long-distance runs. To get into Triumph ownership wholeheartedly, a rider can choose from an extensive range of factory-endorsed garments, kitting him- or herself out with absolutely anything, be it wet- or cold-weather clothing or fashion items. And it's all well made. As far as I'm concerned though, there's a Hein Gericke store in Norwich, while my nearest Triumph outlet is Lings at Watton. Mind you, it's an excuse for a run – as if one were needed!

Two-up and touring, with matching hard luggage fitted, the Sprint ST had sufficient power, torque and handling ability – not to mention comfort – to ride out with the best of them.

Appendix

TRIUMPH DISTRIBUTORS WORLDWIDE

UK
Triumph Motorcycles
Limited
Hinckley, Leicestershire
Tel: +44 1455 251 700
Fax: +44 1455 251 367

Argentina
Moto Mel
Buenos Aires
Tel: +54 1 865 3879
Fax: +54 1 865 3917

Australia
Triumph Australia
Melbourne, Victoria
Tel: +61 3 602 5833
Fax: +61 3 670 2691

Austria
Triumph Deutschland
GmbH
Rosbach vdH
Tel: +49 6003 8981
Fax: +49 6003 8985

Benelux
Greenib. B. V.
HE Warmond
The Netherlands
Tel: +31 1771 19292
Fax: +31 1711 19380

Brazil
Interport
Sao Paulo
Tel: +55 11 22 00 12 29
Fax: +55 11 22 00 12 29

Canada
Triumph Canada
Woodstock
Tel: +506 3288853
Fax: +506 3284608

Cyprus
Fairways
Nicosia
Tel: +357 2 442037
Fax: +357 2 452663

Finland
Vehicletech Trading Oy
Ylimarma
Tel: +358 64 484 6700
Fax: +358 64 484 6960

France
Triumph France
Croissy-Beauborg
Tel: +33 1 64 623838
Fax: +33 1 49 805828

Germany
Triumph Deutschland
GmbH
Rosbach vdH
Tel: +49 6003 8981
Fax: +49 6003 8985

Greece
Triumph Hellas
Athens
Tel: +301 7770079
Fax: +301 7716895

Hong Kong
All Motorcycles
North Point
Tel: +852 887 0498
Fax: +852 807 1246

Israel
P.T.S. Limited
Tel-Aviv
Tel: +972 3 6834106
Fax: +972 3 6826888

Italy
Numero Tre srl
Arese, Milan
Tel: +39 2935 82000
Fax: +39 2935 81933

For a complete listing of Triumph's dealer network worldwide, check the company's website at: www.triumph.co.uk

Japan
Rays Corporation
Osaka
Tel: +81 6 746 1010
Fax: +81 6 746 6652

Kuwait
Desert Star Trading
Company
Safat
Tel: +965 4838101/ 4840076
Fax: +965 4840078

Malaysia
Jayaplus Motor SDN BHD
Kuala Lumpur

Malta
Cycle World Limited
Msida
Tel: +356 313013
Fax: +356 318877

Mexico
Pro-Pisa
Mexico City
Tel: +52 5 554 8081
Fax: +52 5 659 0103

New Zealand
Triumph New Zealand
Auckland
Tel: +649 276 6453
Fax: +649 276 4065

Norway
Power Motorcycles AS
Oslo
Tel: +47 67 53 8562
Fax: +47 67 53 2074

Portugal
ABOL Motors
Lisbon
Tel: +351 1 3159920
Fax: +351 1 3131233

Singapore
Minerva Motor Pte Limited
Singapore
Tel: +65 4722811
Fax: +65 4734968

Sweden
English Motorcycles A.B.
Norsburg
Tel: +46 853 193800
Fax: +46 853 174342

South Africa
Triumph Motorcycles South
Africa
Randburg
Tel: +27 11 7929110
Fax: +27 11 7928100

Spain
Onex SA
Valencia
Tel: +34 6 1521141
Fax: +34 6 1520692

Switzerland
Mohag
Zurich
Tel: +41 1 434 8686
Fax: +41 1 434 806

United Arab Emirates
Gorica Trading
Dubai
Tel: +9714 330659
Fax: +9714 330078

USA
Triumph America
Atlanta, Georgia
Tel: +404 631 9500
Fax: +404 631 6401

Uruguay
Deceleste SA
Montevideo
Tel: +598 294 8848
Fax: +598 294 4229

Zimbabwe
Clarke Marine (PVT)
Limited
Harare
Tel/Fax: +2634 36262

Index

174